SPYING

SPYING

THE MODERN WORLD OF ESPIONAGE

RON FRIDELL

TWENTY-FIRST CENTURY BOOKS
BROOKFIELD, CONNECTICUT

To my father and mother-R.F.

Photographs courtesy of Gamma Presse Images: pp. 24 (© Wilson A. Jamal), 30; Getty Images: pp. 27 (Dan Callister © Online USA, Inc.), 69 (USAF), 127 (Carlos Villalon/Newsmakers); © Corbis: p. 37; MIT Lincoln Laboratory, Lexington, Massachusetts (reprinted with permission): pp. 43, 44; Archive Photos: pp. 55 (Hulton Getty), 88 (Reuters/STR); Sipa Press: p. 77 (© Zoran Mrdja); AP/Wide World Photos: pp. 106, 118

Library of Congress Cataloging-in-Publication Data
Fridell, Ron
Spying : the modern world of espionage / Ron Fridell.
p. cm
Includes bibliographical references and index.
Summary: Examines the types of intelligence gathered by the CIA, the FBI, and the NSA, technological and human resources used to gather such data, and the future of these three organizations.
ISBN 0-7613-1662-0 (lib. bdg.)
1. Intelligence service—United States—Juvenile literature. 2. United States. Central Intelligence Agency—Juvenile literature. 3. United States. Federal Bureau of Investigation—Juvenile literature. 4. United States. National Security Agency—Juvenile literature. [1. Intelligence service. 2. United States. Central Intelligence Agency. 3. United States. Federal Bureau of Investigation. 4. United States. National Security Agency. 5. Spies.] I. Title.
JK468.I6 F75 2002 327.1273—dc21   2001037331

Published by Twenty-First Century Books
A Division of The Millbrook Press, Inc.
2 Old New Milford Road
Brookfield, CT 06804
www.millbrookpress.com

CONTENTS

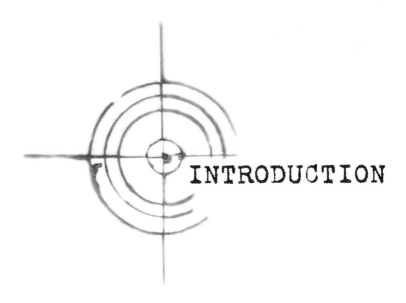

INTRODUCTION

A car pulls into a parking space at the U.S. State Department's C Street headquarters in Washington, D.C. The letter code DYR on the license plates identifies the car as belonging to the Russian embassy. A tall man in a long overcoat gets out and walks a few blocks away to a city park. He sits on a bench facing the State Department and lights up a cigarette.

To the casual observer, the man on the park bench is innocently relaxing on a pleasant spring morning—it is May 1999. Only if you were watching very closely would you notice that the man has slid his hand inside his overcoat.

In a pocket inside the overcoat is a triggering device the size and shape of a TV remote control. By pressing a few buttons, the man activates a bug, a tiny listening device, concealed somewhere in the U.S. State Department building a few blocks away. The bug in the State Department building sends radio signals to a Kleenex box sitting on the car's dashboard. Inside the box, an antenna picks up the bug's signals, and a miniature recorder tapes them.

After a while, the man in the park gets up, walks back to his car, and drives off. Instead of innocently relaxing in the park that morning, Stanislav Gusev, professional spy, was hard at work gathering secret information for the Russian Intelligence Service.

A spy is a person who keeps secret watch on the actions of others. Using this broad definition, nearly everyone has been a spy at one time or another. Children spy on one another for fun. In the adult world, however, spying is serious business, usually done for security and protection. When you enter a subway station, a bank, or a convenience store, chances are a hidden camera takes your picture. In 1998 a block-by-block survey of the Manhattan area of New York City was conducted. The surveyors were looking for hidden surveillance cameras. They identified 2,397, all watching over some street or store or apartment building. If you live in an urban area today, chances are that you are being spied upon by someone somewhere on a daily basis.

In a more specialized sense, a spy is a person who tries to get secret information for one government about another government. This kind of spying is also done for reasons of security—national security. This book is about those kinds of spies, people like Stanislav Gusev; professional spies who do their spying for secret government agencies.

Secret Agencies,
Secret Agents

1

If you know the enemy and know yourself, you need not fear the results of a hundred battles. If you know yourself but not the enemy, for every victory gained you will also suffer a defeat. If you know neither the enemy nor yourself, you will succumb in every battle.

—Sun Tzu[1]

Spying is all about getting to know the enemy. Information about the enemy gathered by professional spies is known as *intelligence*. At the same time that Stanislav Gusev was gathering intelligence on the U.S. government, spies from rival U.S. secret agencies were in Russia gathering intelligence on the Russian government. "Clearly each country has major security concerns about the other," said intelligence expert Steve Aftergood. "We still want to know everything that's going on there, and they want to know everything going on here."[2]

Gathering intelligence by trickery and deception is known as *espionage*. Espionage is the oldest method of gathering intelligence. It has been a part of political and military affairs since the dawn of recorded history. In the *Old Testament* (Numbers 13:17), Moses sends spies into the land of Canaan to gather secret intelligence on the Egyptians. In *The Iliad*, Homer's epic poem of ancient Greece, the Trojans dispatch a spy to the enemy camp to gather military intelligence on the Greeks. In fifth century B.C. China, general and military thinker Sun Tzu encouraged the use of spies to gather intelligence on one's opponents for the purpose of deceiving them. All war, he wrote, is based on deception.

The modern system of espionage was developed during World War II (1939–1945) and the period that followed, known as the Cold War (1945–1991). During World War II, espionage was used by nations directly at war with one another: Britain, France, Russia, and the United States on one side; Germany, Japan, and Italy on the other. During the Cold War, espionage was used by the two superpowers, the United States and the Soviet Union. They never engaged in actual physical combat, a "hot" war. But for nearly a half century they did fight in psychological war, with the two sides spying on each other and accusing each other of attempting to rule the world.

One of the results of these sixty-plus years of "hot" and "cold" warfare is a modern, highly developed system of espionage involving vast and far-reaching communities of secret agencies worldwide. Britain, France, Israel, and Russia are among the nations with the most highly developed intelligence communities. But the United States has by far the largest and most far-reaching of all.

THE INTELLIGENCE COMMUNITY

The U.S. intelligence community is composed of 13 separate federal agencies. The best known are the Federal Bureau of Investigation (FBI), the National Security Agency (NSA), and the Central Intelligence Agency (CIA).

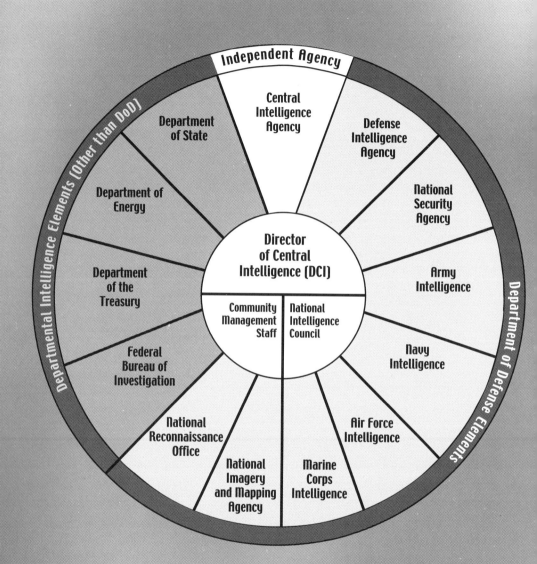

Independent Agency

Central Intelligence Agency

Department of State

Department of Energy

Departmental Intelligence Elements (Other than DoD)

Department of the Treasury

Federal Bureau of Investigation

National Reconnaissance Office

National Imagery and Mapping Agency

Marine Corps Intelligence

Air Force Intelligence

Navy Intelligence

Army Intelligence

Department of Defense Elements

National Security Agency

Defense Intelligence Agency

Director of Central Intelligence (DCI)

Community Management Staff

National Intelligence Council

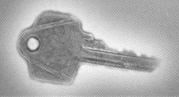

The FBI, headquartered in Washington, D.C., is responsible for detecting and countering foreign intelligence activity within the United States. It was FBI agents who eventually discovered Stanislav Gusev's spying and apprehended him. As of January 2001, the FBI employed some 11,400 special agents and 16,000 support personnel. The agency's budget for fiscal 2001 was $3.57 billion.

The NSA, headquartered in Fort Meade, Maryland, calls itself "the nation's cryptologic organization." It "coordinates, directs, and performs highly specialized activities to protect U.S. information systems and produces foreign intelligence information."[3] In other words, the NSA has two primary missions. The first is to make sure that U.S. secret information remains secret. The second is to gather secret foreign intelligence sent by electromagnetic means, such as phones and computers. And since much foreign intelligence is transmitted in code, the NSA is also responsible for decoding it (code breaking), as well as for encoding U.S. secret information (code making).

The NSA is the most secret secret agency in the U.S. intelligence community, so secret that insiders say its initials ought to stand for "No Such Agency" or "Never Say Anything." The number of NSA employees is a national secret, but security experts estimate that the agency employs about 100,000 people worldwide. The NSA budget is a closely guarded secret.

The CIA is the secret agency responsible for actual spying, conducting espionage operations outside U.S. borders. Security experts estimate that the CIA employs about 20,000 people worldwide and operates on a budget of about $30 billion a year.

CIA INTELLIGENCE OFFICERS

The CIA's espionage activity is conducted like a business, with its own company policies and regulations. CIA intelligence officers, also known as case officers, are the managers, responsible for day-to-day espionage operations in the opponent nation. Their primary job is to recruit, train, and manage secret agents, who do most of the actual spying.

All CIA intelligence officers must be American citizens, and most are men with military experience. They have had at least one year of training at the CIA's training facility, known as "the Farm," at Camp Peary in Williamsburg, Virginia. At "the Farm," candidates learn how to recruit and manage agents. After graduation, the new intelligence officers are sent to their stations. A few are stationed in the United States, where they recruit secret agents employed by foreign embassies or consulates in U.S. cities. But most CIA intelligence officers are stationed in opponent nations overseas.

Espionage is illegal wherever it is practiced. Wherever CIA intelligence officers are stationed overseas, they are operating illegally. This means they must work in secret and under cover. That's why most officers operate with an official cover or identity, such as a U.S. government job that gives them a legal reason to live and work in the opponent nation. Most official covers are positions with the U.S. embassy or consulate.

This official cover also gives officers diplomatic immunity, which is protection from punishment if they are discovered engaging in espionage, or "compromised." With diplomatic immunity, a compromised officer can't be jailed. Instead, the officer is sent home *persona non grata*, a Latin term that translates to "no longer welcome." The United States does the same thing to intelligence officers from other nations who are compromised inside U.S. borders.

Some intelligence officers operate with a non-official cover. These officers run the constant danger of being captured and punished, since a non-official cover does not include diplomatic immunity. Most non-official cover officers operate as U.S. businesspeople, which gives them the chance to meet a variety of potential agents in the opponent nation's business community.

An intelligence officer's primary responsibility is finding potential agents and recruiting them as spies. Recruiting an agent takes time, patience, and extraordinary people skills. It also takes the instincts of a good hunter. After getting acquainted with a potential agent, the officer must work hard at making this person a friend, discovering this person's likes and dislikes, weaknesses and strengths, problems and needs. The officer must also gain this person's trust. And while doing all this, the officer must play a continual cat-and-mouse game, knowing exactly when and how to drop hints about his real intentions without scaring off the object of his hunt. All this can take weeks, months, even years. Finally, the officer stops hinting at his intentions and makes the pitch, proposing that the potential agent turn traitor and become a spy for the United States—a secret agent.

CIA SECRET AGENTS

Secret agents are not officially employed by the CIA, but the CIA pays them to gather secrets about their nation's government, military, and economy, and report them to the CIA officers who recruited them. Since secret agents are insiders—that is, citizens of the host nation—they are in a much better position than intelligence officers to gather secret information.

They are also in a dangerous position. Secret agents must operate without the protection of diplomatic immunity; and by spying for the enemy, they are betraying their own nation. Branded as traitors, compromised agents are generally dealt with harshly. Some have been executed.

Most secret agents are high-level employees of the opponent nation's government. Some are the opponent nation's intelligence officers. Their jobs give them believable reasons for meeting and mixing with officials of their own government and other potential sources of intelligence.

Other secret agents are lower-level government employees, such as chauffeurs, secretaries, janitors, and night watchmen.

These lower-level spies have the advantage of being relatively invisible. They are less likely than their higher-level counterparts to be suspected of being spies.

SPYING FOR REVENGE

Why spy?

Most secret agents become spies for the money. As a rule, espionage pays well. Some agents have made millions.

But money is not the only motive. Ego sometimes plays a part. Some secret agents crave contact with the intrigue and adventure associated with spying. Becoming a part of the mysterious world of espionage feeds their ego, their need to see themselves as uncommon persons, living above the crowd.

For others, revenge is a motive. They spy as a way of getting back at civilian bosses or military officers whom they feel have treated them unfairly. Albert Sombolay, an American soldier who fought in the 1991 Gulf War, passed secret information about U.S. troop readiness to a Jordanian intelligence officer in exchange for $1,300. He did this, he said, because his U.S. Army superiors had reduced his rank as a punishment for breaking rules. Sombolay was caught spying by U.S. military intelligence officers. After pleading guilty to charges of espionage and aiding the enemy, Sombolay was sentenced to 19 years at hard labor.

SPYING FOR A CAUSE

Some people become spies out of personal political conviction. Mordechai Vanunu, former senior nuclear technician in a secret Israeli nuclear plant, became a spy in the name of world peace. He leaked highly classified information concerning Israel's nuclear activities to the London *Sunday Times*, which published them in 1986. Vanunu's thinking went this way: Israel's nuclear weapons program was too successful, and this success had turned Israel into such a powerful military force that it now posed a dire threat to world peace. With so much tension between Israel and its Middle Eastern neighbors, Vanunu feared that Israel would attack its neighbors with nuclear weapons. He thought that by making some of Israel's nuclear secrets public, he could diminish its lead in the nuclear-arms race and thereby make a nuclear attack less likely.

In the eyes of his government, though, the well-meaning Vanunu was one of the most notorious traitors in history. After his capture by Israeli Special Services agents in London, Vanunu was put in chains and brought back to Israel, where he was found guilty of treason, espionage, and the passing of state secrets, and sentenced to 18 years in prison.

FAMILY TIES

Other people turn to spying because of strong family ties. This is especially true in the United States, where so many citizens have close relatives in other nations. The case of George Trofimoff shows how strong and long-lasting these family ties can be. Trofimoff was born of Russian parents, and became a naturalized U.S. citizen in 1951. After serving in the Army Reserve, he became an Army intelligence officer. In the late 1960s, Trofimoff became a spy for America's chief Cold War opponent, the Soviet Union. He was recruited as a spy by a boyhood friend, a Russian.

One important intelligence mission is to find out what your opponent knows about you. In this regard, Trofimoff helped the Russians greatly. From 1969 to 1994 he sold them classified documents detailing secret information that the U.S. government had obtained concerning Soviet nuclear-weapons capabilities. Trofimoff photographed these classified documents in his office in Nuremberg, Germany, where he was stationed as a civilian Army employee. This was his non-official cover. During these 25 years of spying, the Soviets paid him over $250,000.

In July 1997, Trofimoff was compromised by a U.S. undercover agent posing as a Russian intelligence officer. During a meeting with the undercover agent, Trofimoff admitted selling secrets to the Russians. A videotape captured him putting his hand over his heart and declaring, "I'm not American in here," meaning that while officially a U.S. citizen, in his heart of hearts Trofimoff remained loyal to his motherland, Russia.

AGENTS UNDER PRESSURE

Finally, there is the use of pressure. Intelligence officers want to recruit agents who are willing to sell them information. Willing spies are more apt to remain loyal than spies recruited by force. But sometimes officers resort to applying pressure, more and more of it, until the potential spy caves in. The process begins when an intelligence officer finds a weakness in a potential agent. Former FBI intelligence director Pat Watson said, "When a Russian comes to the United States, we immediately start looking at him for recruitment. Anything that pops up on the screen that shows he has a problem, we are going to attempt to exploit that."[4]

The kinds of problems that Watson refers to often involve sex or money, which makes these potential agents vulnerable to blackmail. Some are set up to be secretly photographed accepting money from an intelligence officer or in the company of a prostitute. Then they are shown the photographs and told that if they do not cooperate, their employers and families will be shown the evidence.

Major Sergei Motorin, a young Soviet intelligence officer, provides an example of what can happen to a potential agent under pressure. Stationed at the Soviet Embassy in Washington, D.C., Motorin was assigned to collect political intelligence under the cover of being a Soviet embassy employee. When U.S. intelligence officers learned that Motorin, a married man, was having extramarital affairs, they saw a weakness to exploit.

Motorin had violated a cardinal rule of espionage: He had made himself vulnerable through weakness of character. CIA

officers confronted Motorin and threatened to tell his superiors about his affairs. If they did, they reminded him, he cer-
tainly would lose his job and, perhaps, his family as well.
Motorin caved in to this blackmail and turned over to the FBI
the name of every Soviet intelligence officer operating undercover in the Soviet Embassy in Washington.

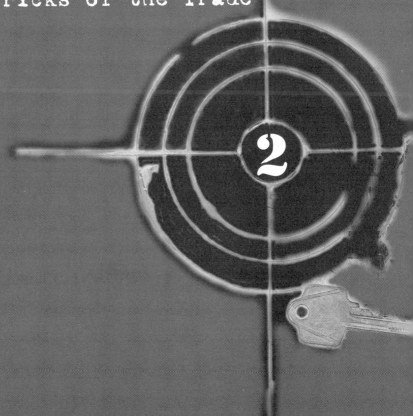

Spies at Work:
Tricks of the Trade

2

During the Revolutionary War, General George Washington wrote to one of his men about the value of intelligence support in a coming attack against the British. The letter emphasized the one thing without which spies cannot operate.

> The necessity for procuring good intelligence is apparent and need not be further urged—all that remains for me to add is, that you keep the whole matter as secret as possible. For upon Secrecy, Success depends in most enterprises of the kind, and for want of it, they are generally defeated, however well planned and promising a favorable issue.[1]

Today, the techniques spies use to gather and pass secret information are known as *tradecraft*.

SECRET MEETINGS

Agents must somehow pass the intelligence they have collected over to their handler, an intelligence officer. When this is done in a face-to-face meeting, crowded public places such as city parks and shopping malls are often used. They are easily reached anonymously, by public transportation, and a person can escape detection if necessary by melting into the crowd.

An agent may use a deliberately circuitous route to get to the meeting place. He may take a bus or subway going north, for instance, then immediately take another one going in the opposite direction. This gives him time to check for surveillance, to see if he is being tailed. On the other hand, his adversaries may know what he's up to and switch tails along the way, having a new follower take the place of the old one. To be a secret agent is to live in an atmosphere of constant suspicion. No matter how cautious you are, you can never be one-hundred-percent sure that you're not being watched.

The actual physical exchange of information is accomplished with the same high degree of secrecy and caution. Sometimes it's a matter of the agent sitting down at the handler's table in a mall food court with a shopping bag identical to the handler's, then walking off with the handler's bag and leaving his own bag containing the intelligence for the handler to take away. Sometimes it's a matter of simply slipping an envelope into the handler's hand as they pass on the street, called a "brush pass."

DEAD DROPS

To avoid face-to-face meetings, agents sometimes drop off their information at a prearranged site, so that a short time later, the handler may come and pick it up. These sites are known as dead drops. Successfully executing a dead drop exchange demands careful planning, precise timing, and a bit of luck. Drop sites are chosen carefully and changed often. Sites must be inconspicuous but also easy to find and visible from several different perspectives. That way both agent and handler can survey the site from a distance to make sure that no one is watching.

This photograph, released by the FBI, shows the dead drop site used by former FBI agent Robert Hanssen. He tucked his packages under this footbridge, which offered the combination of an identifiable place of concealment in a relatively open area so he could make sure he was alone.

The procedure for making a dead drop involves a series of signals. Chalk marks, for example, may be left by the handler on telephone poles or park benches along the way. If the proper marks are in place, the agent proceeds with the drop. If not, he knows the drop is off and turns back.

Containers for drops are also carefully chosen and placed. If the intelligence to be delivered consists of something small, such as a roll of microfilm, an empty aluminum soft drink can left next to a tree is sometimes used. Since aluminum recycling began, though, this method isn't used as often, because the can could be accidentally picked up by a passing salvager. Other dead drop containers include drain pipes, dumpsters, and holes in tree trunks.

Some highly inventive containers have been used. One intelligence officer in a Central European city is said to have used the hollowed-out carcasses of dead rats for a while, until he found that they didn't always work. Cats sometimes ate his containers, and the secret agent's intelligence along with them.

Not all dead drop operations are successful. John Walker, Jr., an employee of the U.S. Department of Defense, operated a spy ring selling naval communications secrets to the Soviets. Walker's ex-wife and daughter tipped off the FBI, who then began following Walker. They were watching from concealed spots along a remote country road in Maryland one morning when Walker arrived and placed a soda can at the foot of a roadside utility pole. Walker was also carrying a garbage bag, which he carefully placed behind a neighboring utility pole.

After Walker moved on, FBI agents came out of concealment and removed the can, which was empty. A short time later, Walker's handler, a Soviet intelligence officer, arrived on the scene. When he saw that the signal to pick up the secret documents, the soda can, was not at the foot of the utility pole, he retreated and returned to the Soviet Embassy in Washington. FBI agents then removed the garbage bag, which contained the secret documents intended for Walker's Soviet handler. Walker was arrested later that day. He was eventually sentenced to two life terms in prison.

SPY CAMERAS

Agents use high-tech cameras and listening devices to gather secret intelligence. Micro videocameras smaller than a postage stamp have been hidden in the most unlikely spots. They have been fitted into the ceilings of passenger planes, pointed downward, so that when the passenger below opens a folder, the camera records the documents as the passenger looks them over. They have been installed in smoke detectors and light fixtures. Even wall clocks have been used, with the lens looking out the tiny screw hole where the hands of the clock are joined. Miniature mobile spy cameras have been installed on spies themselves in equally ingenious ways. An agent's button may actually be taking pictures. So may the knot in his necktie or the frames of his eyeglasses or a looseleaf notebook or matchbox.

Night-vision equipment makes it possible to take pictures even in candlelit rooms. A lit cigarette gives enough of a glow for an image-intensifier camera to pick up a picture of the smoker's face. Besides night-vision cameras, spies may also use night-vision goggles to see in near-darkness. Worn with a thick harness that clips around the head, the goggles create a kind of greenish daylight view of things. An infrared flashlight can be used to make the view more distinct, because it casts a bright light on a totally dark scene that only the spy, wearing the goggles, can see.

LISTENING DEVICES

Agents use bugs to record secret information. Some bugs are stationary, like the one used by Soviet spy Stanislav Gusev, which was concealed in the State Department building. Stationary bugs can be hidden in plants, electrical outlets, furniture, and even in pictures hung on walls.

One of the most famous bugs in espionage history was known as "The Thing." In the early years of the Cold War, during the 1950s, the Soviets made what American officials

A built-in camera in these sunglasses is transmitting the image seen on the screen in the background. These sunglasses are sold in a popular retail spy store in Beverly Hills, California.

assumed was a goodwill gesture. They presented a special gift to the American ambassador in Moscow, the former Soviet Union's capital city. The gift was a wood carving of the Great Seal of the United States. (The Great Seal, which has an eagle inside it, can be seen on the back of a dollar bill.) The carving looked quite impressive mounted on the wall above the ambassador's desk, where it remained for a number of years.

When the Americans finally realized that intelligence was being leaked from the ambassador's office, they took "The Thing" apart and found an ingenious metal cylinder 8 inches (20 centimeters) long. It had no wires or batteries, but a spring inside the cylinder vibrated whenever anyone nearby spoke, and Soviet spies in a building outside the embassy were able to pick up these vibrations with radar.

Portable listening devices such as microphones, transmitters, and recorders have been concealed in belt buckles, wristwatches, and pens. They have been found in the soles of diplomats' shoes and the spines of books. You can buy these high-tech espionage devices yourself, in stores and over the Internet. The Super Ear Microphone captures conversations from 200 feet (60 meters) away. The Wall Probe Transmitter pressed to the wall allows the listener to hear conversations inside the next room. The Fake Ink Pen Microphone "appears to be an attractive Ink Pen," the ad says. "However, looks are deceiving. The top of this pen contains a high-quality microphone. From the bottom of the pen extends a wire which will easily connect to a recorder."[2] The price is $99.95.

WATCHING AGENTS

While these hide-and-seek tactics and high-tech gadgets give espionage an intriguing look and feel, it is not as inviting an occupation as it may seem. For intelligence officers, an important part of spy tradecraft is keeping a sharp eye on the mental state of the agents. Since agents engage in an ongoing game of deception and betrayal, they are liable to experience an intense sense of isolation and guilt that can lead to depression and despair.

Here, for example, is how two agents convicted of espionage against America look back on their years of spying. Harry Gold, a secret agent for the Soviet Union, remembers "the many lies I had to tell at home, and to my friends, to explain my whereabouts during these absences from home. Mom was certain that I was carrying on a series of clandestine [secret] love affairs, and nothing could have been farther from the truth. The hours of waiting on street corners, waiting dubiously and fearfully in strange towns where I had no business to be. . ."[3] The second agent, Bin Wu, was recruited by the Chinese secret service to emigrate to the United States and spy for China. In 1993, after he was compromised, tried, and convicted, Wu was sentenced to ten years in prison by the United States. Speaking of how he felt during his years as a spy, Wu said, "The world is topsy-turvy, jumbled and confused. I get a cold feeling to know the sky is empty and nobody is there watching."[4]

Officers must also keep a close watch on their agents' loyalty, which may turn at any time. Secret agents' motives and reliability are always in doubt. Having already betrayed their own nation, they could easily turn around and betray the intelligence officer and his or her nation.

Agents may secretly turn against their handlers by feeding them false information. Some intelligence officers have been deceived by a scam called "running a paper mill." When double agents run paper mills, they deliberately supply misinformation meant to mislead the opponent nation. The agent supplies the officer with "secret" documents, which in fact the agent has created himself. The agent may be "running a paper mill" because he can't actually gain access to the intelligence he's being paid to gather, or he may be a double agent, secretly working against the nation he has been hired to work for.

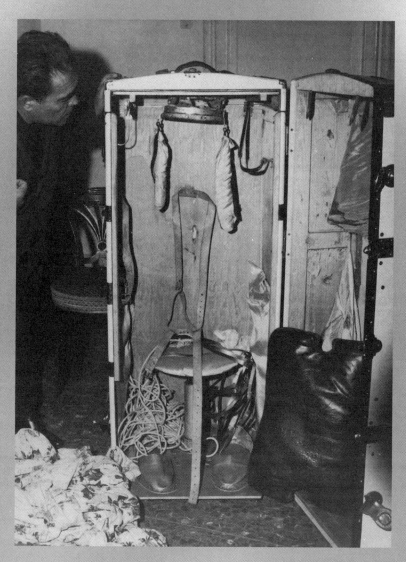

This elaborate trunk was built around 1950 to transport a spy to Cairo, Egypt, from Italy. He was discovered before the flight.

PROTECTING AGENTS

Many secret agents do remain loyal to their handlers, and intelligence officers must be prepared to protect them. In espionage, as in any other business, it makes good sense to take good care of your employees. If you don't, you may find that no one is willing to work for you. Since secret agents are exposed to so much potential danger, they must feel confident that their handlers are taking good care of them.

This is where another important aspect of tradecraft comes into play: *exfiltration*. Exfiltration is the opposite of infiltration. It means secretly removing a person from a dangerous situation before that person can be harmed. A secret agent without benefit of diplomatic immunity, a secret agent caught in his own country is certain to be punished, perhaps even tortured or killed. Good intelligence officers keep an exfiltration plan in place in case an agent should fall under suspicion or, worse, become compromised.

All exfiltration plans involve danger, and some demand especially ingenious strategies for dealing with this danger. One agent, for example, was successfully driven to safety in a specially designed car. The driveshaft in a Land Rover had been removed from its customary middle position and repositioned to the side of the car. The compromised agent was hidden in a special compartment in the bump down the middle where the driveshaft should have been, and unsuspecting border guards let the car through. Most exfiltration plans involve either hiding or disguising the agent as he is being smuggled out of the country to safety. The CIA's Technical Services Division in the United States designs special disguises and escape plans and equipment for use in exfiltration schemes.

THE HUMAN ELEMENT

Personality, character, brains, and courage all play important parts in the human side of espionage. So do carelessness and poor judgment. Espionage involves the manipulation of people who are potential sources of information, and people don't always react as expected. No matter how sophisticated the technical gadgets or how carefully laid out the plans, things can go wrong when people under pressure try to steal secrets. It is the intelligence officer's job to deal with these potential problems. To run his operation successfully, an officer must be a shrewd judge of character. And the officer and agent both must be good at thinking on their feet and rolling with the punches. If not, they will not be engaged in espionage for long.

Spies in
the Sky

3

The time is December 1999. The place is outer space. A U.S. spy satellite orbits the Earth some 423 miles (681 kilometers) above North Korea. The satellite gathers electronic signals, which are then beamed down to a collecting station on the ground. Computers translate the signals to show images of Rodong, a top-secret North Korean missile base. Sixteen months earlier a long-range missile was test-fired from this base, aimed south and east over Japan and into the Pacific Ocean beyond.

The modern Communist state of North Korea is a closed society, much like the Soviet Union during the Cold War years. The North Korean government controls the information that goes out over its national media, and it is notoriously careful about keeping its military capabilities secret. No one from the news media is allowed anywhere near Rodong.

North Korea's relations with the United States are sometimes openly hostile. This fact, coupled with rumors of new activity at Rodong, has raised U.S. concerns. Are the North Koreans in the process of developing long-range missiles with nuclear warheads? Could the secret missile base at Rodong pose a threat to the United States?

The images from the spy satellite were analyzed by intelligence experts. These experts measured the sizes of the structures and the distances between them and described their possible functions. Then these satellite images, together with analysts' descriptions, were released to the president and key members of his Cabinet and Congress. The Rodong images were of vital importance. A heated debate was in progress during 1999 and 2000 over whether the U.S. Congress should allot $60 billion for a new anti-missile defense system (NMD).

The Rodong images supplied ammunition for people on both sides of the issue. Those against the NMD focused on what was missing from the picture. They pointed out how crude the Rodong base appeared to be. How could supplies be brought in when no paved roads or rail lines appeared in any of the spy satellite images? And where were the fuel tanks? Where was the staff housing that would have to be in place to support a major program for manufacturing and testing long-range missiles?

Those in favor of the NMD looked at those same Rodong images with a different eye, a different mindset. Instead of what was missing, they focused on what was there. They pointed out that the single launchpad, control facility, and the building for assembling missiles posed a genuine threat. Former Pentagon official Frank J. Gaffney, Jr., said that American officials would be "fools to ignore capabilities that have the potential to do us grave harm."[1]

THE RISE OF TECHINT

The images collected by the spy satellite over Rodong are an example of technology intelligence, or *Techint*, intelligence gathered using the latest technology in place of human agents. The importance of Techint rose dramatically during the Cold War years. The Soviet Union was fanatical about keeping all information about itself secret from its primary opponent, the United States. Traditional open sources of information, such as newspapers and television and radio, were under strict government control. And the movements of the few Americans permitted to visit the Soviet Union were closely watched.

So the United States had to go to great lengths to steal Soviet secrets. The CIA developed an extensive network of intelligence officers and secret agents—the *Humint* factor. And the CIA, NSA, and other members of the U.S. intelligence community kept developing more sophisticated technical devices for collecting information from greater and greater distances, the Techint factor.

Techint components include spy satellites, manned and unmanned spy planes, and land- and sea-based listening posts. Using Techint devices to collect visual intelligence is known as *Imint* (image intelligence).

THE RISE OF IMINT

Aerial reconnaissance is the collection of Imint from aircraft. Some of the first aerial reconnaissance was actually done during the American Civil War. In 1862, General McLellan's Union Army used hot-air balloonists to spy on Confederate Army positions during a series of battles known as the siege of Richmond. This was a cumbersome process, using large, heavy cameras positioned in the balloon baskets to capture shaky photos of the enemy.

Airplanes were used to gather Imint on a regular basis during World War I (1914–1918). Much of this war was fought in trenches, long lines of ditches dug deep to protect and house soldiers at the front, where the actual hand-to-hand fighting took place. In February 1915, Britain's Royal Air Force used Imint to discover the existence of a hidden German trench system. The British and French had planned an assault on the German Army in the area where the trench system was discovered. This intelligence about the hidden trenches changed their plans. Knowing that the Germans would be well fortified and ready for them, the British and French armies called off what likely would have been an ill-fated assault.

Aerial reconnaissance continued during World War II (1939–1945). More sophisticated planes and cameras gathered

Mathew Brady, who used his camera to document the Civil War, took this photograph of the hot-air balloon *Intrepid* about to be launched for a spying mission.

intelligence from higher altitudes to avoid antiaircraft fire. The resulting Imint was used to identify bombing targets and assess the resulting damage.

Special spy planes were developed during the Cold War years for the purpose of taking ultra-high-altitude photographs of the Soviet Union. One of the most successful spy planes was the U-2. Its huge wingspan of 103 feet (30.9 meters) and extreme lightness at 40,000 pounds (18,000 kilograms) allowed it to fly at an altitude of more than 70,000 feet (21,212 meters).[2] This was high enough to keep it from being shot down by Soviet antiaircraft weapons. The U-2 missions were dedicated to gathering images of military installations and missile bases.

The last U-2 mission took place on May 1, 1960, when a newly developed Soviet surface-to-air missile shot a U-2 out of the air. Pilot Francis Gary Powers parachuted to safety and was captured by the Soviets. After Powers confessed to espionage, President Dwight Eisenhower was forced to admit that the United States had been illegally flying over Soviet airspace, and the U-2 was withdrawn from service.

U.S. spy planes equipped with advanced radar-surveillance devices continue to fly intelligence-gathering missions today. One mission led to a serious encounter between the U.S. and Chinese governments. On April 1, 2001, a U.S. Navy surveillance plane on a flight off the coast of China collided with a Chinese fighter plane. The Chinese plane crashed into the sea, killing the pilot. The U.S. plane plunged 8,000 feet (2,440 meters) before the Navy pilot managed to bring it under control. The damaged plane then made an emergency landing on the Chinese island of Hainan. All 24 crew members survived.

While the damaged Navy plane descended, crew members destroyed secret computer software and data files that would have been of great value to the Chinese government. But the crew could not destroy the secret radar and surveillance devices built into the aircraft.

Armed Chinese guards surrounded the spy plane when it landed, and escorted the U.S. crew out at gunpoint. The next day Chinese military technicians flew to Hainan Island to study the plane. The Chinese released the 24 American service personnel on April 12, but kept the plane for further study.

Chinese officials demanded that the United States apologize for causing the death of the Chinese pilot, but the it refused, claiming that the Chinese pilot may have been at fault. Chinese officials also suggested that the United States discontinue the spy flights. The United States did suspend the flights following the crash, but resumed them six weeks later.

EARLY SPY SATELLITES

While the U-2 was flying airborne reconnaissance missions in the late 1950s, spy satellites equipped with cameras were being developed for spaceborne reconnaissance. This was the job of the National Reconnaissance Office (NRO), an agency of the U.S. Department of Defense. The NRO is responsible for the research, development, production, and day-to-day operation of spy satellites.

The first successful launch of a U.S. spy satellite took place the year before the U-2 was shot down. On August 19, 1959, *Discoverer XIV* was launched into space. Early spy satellites like *Discoverer* recorded images on film and sent them back to Earth in capsules attached to parachutes. *Discoverer*'s first capsule of film, 20 pounds (7.5 kilograms) of it, was snatched from midair by an Air Force C-119 aircraft as it fell toward Earth. The resulting images, while not as sharp as U-2 photographs, revealed areas of the Soviet Union never before photographed. Soon, improved satellite cameras sent back sharper, more detailed Imint.

NEW KINDS OF IMAGES

The next big leap in spaceborne reconnaissance was the development of digital electro-optical images. Instead of being recorded on film as pictures, electro-optical images are recorded as electrical signals, or data streams, which the satellite transmits to Earth. Each of these signals is assigned a numerical value. These numbered signals are called pixels, or picture elements. The image is constructed from these individual pixels.

Modern spy satellite Imint consists of electro-optical images. Modern satellites are also equipped with infrared imagery technology (IR). Standard electro-optical images require sunlight and clear skies, while IR can produce images of the Earth's surface at any time of the day or night in clear or cloudy conditions. IR works by detecting heat. This means that spy satellites can detect buried structures such as underground buildings and missile silos from the heat given off by the machinery underground.

Early satellite spy photos captured images so detailed that they could show the difference between a Guernsey cow and a Hereford. Modern satellite systems can picture objects the size of a grapefruit, and even smaller, in sharp detail, looking down from more than 400 miles (645 kilometers) above the Earth.

PRIVATE ENTERPRISE

Back in the Cold War years, U.S. intelligence agencies did their own research and development of Imint technology, from night-vision goggles to spy satellites. This practice changed during the 1990s, when private corporations began developing Imint technologies on their own. In some cases their work equaled and even surpassed government-produced technologies.

In December 1999, Space Imaging Corporation of Thornton, Colorado, became the first private corporation to launch a commercial space satellite equipped with Imint technology. Named IKONOS, this satellite orbits Earth 423 miles (681 kilometers) up, passing over nearly any spot on Earth every third morning. IKONOS reportedly is capable of providing images nearly as sharp and powerful as government spy satellites. These images are for sale to individuals, businesses, and government agencies. IKONOS proved so effective that American intelligence agencies began using it to supplement their own spy satellite Imint. The National Imagery Mapping

Agency (NIMA), which is responsible for collecting and distributing Imint, budgeted $500 million for the purchase of satellite imagery from private industry between 2000 and 2005.

UNMANNED AERIAL VEHICLES

Closer to Earth, a new kind of spy plane is being used to gather Imint. Unmanned aerial vehicles (UAVs), also known as drones, are pilotless aircraft guided by earthbound technicians using remote-control devices. Some UAVs can remain over targets for up to 24 hours at a time while sending back a continuous stream of electro-optical imagery via satellite relay. UAVs have two distinct advantages over spy satellites and piloted spy planes: They are relatively cheap to produce, around $10 million each, and involve no risk of human life.

Two UAVs presently in use are DarkStar and Predator. Predator was first used in 1995, when the United States sent peacekeeping teams to the Eastern European country of Bosnia, in the former Yugoslavia, where a bloody civil war was raging. Electro-optical imaging equipment aboard Predator, flying at an altitude of 26,000 feet, produced images so sharp that an area as small as one square foot could be seen in detail. Predator Imint gave U.S. forces vital information on troop and supply movements in Bosnia. The UAV known as DarkStar, also in use, can be completely controlled, from take off to landing, by a small team of computer programmers.

Other UAVs are being developed and tested. One, the Global Hawk, is designed to fly at altitudes greater than 60,000 feet (18,288 meters) and to hover over a designated target for more than 24 hours at a time.

MICRO-UAVS

A number of micro-UAVs are also in development. If they can be made to work as designed, these UAVs will carry Imint capabilities to an astonishing new level. One of these micro-UAVs is Robofly, being developed by a research team at the

University of California at Berkeley. A government agency known as DARPA (Defense Advanced Research Projects Agency) has put $2.5 million into funding Robofly research, with a goal of having it airborne by 2004.

According to plans, Robofly should be roughly the weight and size of a housefly. But unlike a fly, it will have two pairs of wings and only one eye, a sensor for recording electro-optical images. Its body will be made of paper-thin stainless steel and its wings of Mylar, a substance with the look and feel of plastic wrap. Instead of a motor or batteries, it will be run by a tiny device known as a piezoelectric actuator, which is powered by the sun. The actuator will flap Robofly's two pairs of wings at 180 times per second.

If Robofly can be made to work, humans will have learned how to artificially reproduce insect flight. The method behind the development of Robofly comes from biometrics, a field of science in which scientists work at reverse-engineering the workings of nature. They begin with the living housefly itself and study its makeup and movements in extreme detail, all the way down to the microscopic level. From these studies they hope to learn how a fly flies in such detail that they can actually reproduce insect flight using manufactured parts.

Why are these research scientists spending money, time, and effort to mimic insect flight? The answer lies in the relentless quest of modern technology to make things smaller and smaller. Imint is now gathered by conventional-size planes, so the next step is to gather it with miniature aircraft, and the more miniature the better. But the aerodynamic principles used to keep airplanes aloft stop working at a scale as miniature as an insect's. Different principles are at work here, principles the Berkeley scientists hope to discover and put to practical use.

Why are scientists researching a housefly instead of some other insect? Flies can change course in 30-thousandths of a second. They are capable of processing information at astonishing speed. And, as Robofly scientists point out, they can take off and land in virtually any direction, including upside

CAMERA LAYOUT

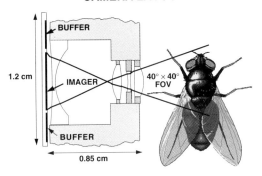

APERTURE	0.26 cm
ANGULAR RESOLUTION	0.7 mrad (7 cm at 100 m Range)
PIXEL COUNT	1000 × 1000
FRAME RATE	0.5 fps
MASS	< 1 GRAM
POWER	< 25 mW

100 m ALTITUDE, 45° ASPECT
40° × 40° TOTAL FOV
1000 × 1000 pix; 4-BIT GRAYSCALE

The publisher was unable to obtain permission to reprint a photograph of Robofly here. This schematic for a miniature visible light camera, also being developed by DARPA, uses a housefly for size comparison.

down. "They're the fighter jets of the animal world," says Ron Fearing, head of the Robofly project.[3]

Another unmanned aerial vehicle in development is the Black Widow, also a DARPA project. Engineers at AeroVironment Inc. in Simi Valley, California, are developing this disk-wing airplane, which measures 6 inches (15 centimeters) across and weighs only 2 ounces (57 grams). The Black Widow was the first micro-UAV to leave the ground. The plane is stored in a small carrying-case, which also carries a control console. Using special goggles, the operator can view live video images from the plane's tiny camera. Officials at the Department of Defense hope that the Black Widow will eventually serve as a tiny spy plane that small combat units can use to search nearby terrain without risking human life.

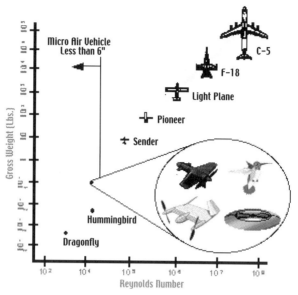

The three UAVs in the oval show some of the UAV shapes that scientists are experimenting with, and their sizes compared to a hummingbird. Also under study are the advantages of remote versus self-piloted versions, and various power sources.

With Imint technology such as Robofly and the Black Widow available, the possibilities for collecting secret intelligence become more and more intriguing. How far has Imint come since its early days? Compare these two pictures in your mind. Imagine the American Civil War soldiers in a hot air balloon being blown about while struggling to steady their cumbersome cameras mounted on wooden tripods as they attempt to take faraway pictures of the battlefield below. That was in 1862. Now imagine what appears to be a tiny fly circling a modern battlefield, unnoticed by the soldiers below but instantly observing their every move, moment to moment, day and night. The differences between these two pictures give us an idea of how much Imint has changed in roughly the last 140 years.

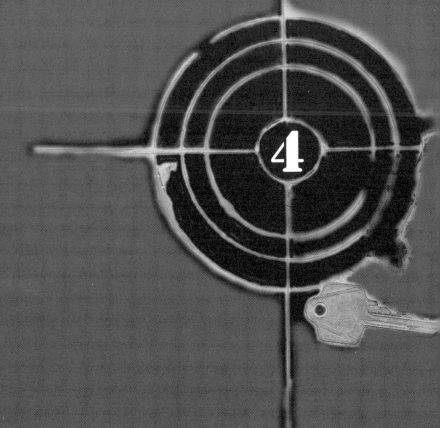

Electronic Eavesdropping:
Comint, Echelon, and
the World Wide Web

4

Sometime during the 1990s (the exact time, place, and other details are government secrets), a U.S. ambassador found himself and his family in a life-threatening situation. Suddenly, civil war had broken out in the ambassador's host nation. Intelligence officers had a secret exfiltration plan in place to get him and his family safely out of the country, but this plan was no longer a secret. Enemy intelligence had gotten hold of it, and a team of assassins waited along the planned escape route.

The ambassador and his family would have run straight into a fatal trap if U.S. intelligence officers had not intercepted a radio message revealing that the assassins were lying in wait, intending to kill everyone. Instead, the ambassador and his family took another exfiltration route and escaped the country safely.

COMINT

The U.S. ambassador and his family were saved by communications intelligence (Comint). Comint, as defined by the National Security Agency, is intelligence "derived from foreign communications by other than their intended recipient."[1] The NSA is responsible for intercepting and analyzing Comint to detect any potential threats to U.S. national security.

Like Imint, Comint depends heavily on satellites. The same spy satellites that produce images also intercept wireless transmission of telephone and computer data and relay them to ground stations on Earth for analysis. For instance, drug dealers in Colombia and the United States setting up a drug deal by cell phone might have their plans intercepted and sent to U.S. counternarcotics agents, who would then use this secret intelligence to intercept the drugs as they arrived in the United States from Colombia.

These interceptions are made possible by microwave spillage. Cell-phone conversations consist of radio signals relayed by microwave stations. These radio signals travel in straight lines. If the Earth were flat, they could be sent anyplace directly. But because of the curvature of the Earth, radio signals must be sent from station to station around the curved Earth. Long-distance cell phone calls may need dozens of these stations to carry the conversations from a person on one continent to a person on another. Each station picks up only a tiny fraction of the signal that reaches it before relaying it to the next station. The rest of the signal, the unused part, passes over the horizon and out into space, where satellites can intercept this microwave spillage and turn it into intelligence.

INTERCEPTING COMINT

Just how far-reaching is Comint? No one really knows, since the U.S. government keeps so much information about intelligence operations secret, but people are always speculating. Ever since the 1970s rumors had been circulating about a worldwide surveillance network enabling government agencies to pick up virtually all telephone and cable communications. These speculations began gathering credibility when news of an operation known as Project Echelon surfaced in the mid-1990s. Finally, in 1999, the governments involved in the project admitted that Project Echelon had been in existence since the 1970s.

Echelon is the code name for a worldwide surveillance network run by the NSA and its intelligence partners in Britain, Australia, Canada, and New Zealand. Echelon's purpose is to give these nations access to all of the world's electronic communications. Echelon has been compared to a vast vacuum cleaner, relentlessly sucking up every last bit of the world's electronic information. Echelon links supercomputers in at least seven sites around the world, which receive, analyze, and sort information beamed down to the supercomputers from spy satellites that capture this information through microwave spillage. In addition, military planes specially equipped to gather electronic communications are constantly in the air, and ground sites all over the world are positioned to do the same. Reportedly, Echelon can intercept a million communications from around the world every half hour.

SELECTING COMINT

How can this massive volume of intercepted information be turned into useful intelligence? The process begins with optical character recognition (OCR) programs. These are computer programs that look for certain code words or phrases. OCR programs work like computer search engines, where you type in a key word or phrase and the search engine presents you with a list of documents from various Web sites that contain that key word or phrase.

Computers at the Echelon ground sites run OCR programs. These computers are known as dictionaries, because each one is programmed with a unique set of key words and phrases. Each U.S. intelligence agency has its own OCR dictionary with its own set of key words and phrases, also known as a watch list, and its own Echelon computer dedicated exclusively to its needs. A typical watch list will include names of people and places, topics of interest, addresses, and telephone numbers. Together, these OCR dictionaries, which change from day to day, amount to a catalogue of the ever-changing missions and targets of secret agencies in terms of military, political, and economic intelligence.

Each key word or phrase represents a request for intelligence. Whenever an OCR dictionary computer receives a message containing a key word or phrase on its watch list, it automatically forwards that message to the requesting agency. Since each agency has its own watch list, each agency receives a different set of intercepted messages every day.

THE ECHELON INFORMATION GLUT

Echelon is said to be capable of intercepting every single e-mail message and cell phone call in the world. A day's worth of satellite telephone calls in the Middle East alone runs into the millions. John C. Gannon, former Deputy Director for Intelligence, said, "The revolution in information technologies has improved our access to sources and our ability to quickly deliver intelligence. But it has also made our work more challenging as we are bombarded with information of varying quality, relevance, and depth."[2]

Of course, most of these messages will be filtered out. According to William Studeman, former NSA director, during a typical half hour, a million intercepted messages are passed on to Echelon computers. The OCR dictionary programs typically filter out all but 6,500, with only 1,000 of these 6,500 surviving a second filtering process. So a total of 1,000 surviving messages are sent along to the appropriate agencies every half hour.[3]

Of these 1,000, no more than ten are typically selected by analysts to be put into an intelligence report. Filtering the 1,000 down to ten is the final step. The first steps, the filtering from a million to 1,000, are done in a matter of minutes by supercomputers. But computers cannot make sense of the messages that remain; only humans can.

But no human can analyze messages at the rate that a computer can. As a result, unanalyzed messages accumulate at a rate far faster than analysts can deal with. Jerry Nelson, a physicist involved in spy satellite work, said, "The information coming down from these satellites is just going to choke you. You can't buy big enough computers to process it. You can't buy enough programmers to write the codes or look at the results to interpret them. At some point you just get saturated."[4]

This saturation point has been reached. Analysts struggle in vain to deal with the glut of information pouring in from Echelon sources. According to William Studeman, in the future, "Information management will be the single most important problem for the U.S. intelligence community."[5]

HUMINT VERSUS TECHINT

Echelon illustrates the increasing importance of Techint in intelligence gathering since the 1990s. It also illustrates the limits of Techint. Echelon supplies an overload of information. Without people to evaluate and make sense of it, this information is of little use. No matter how powerful Techint becomes, it cannot replace the human element. President Bill Clinton said, "No matter how good our technology, we'll always rely on human intelligence to tell us what an adversary has in mind. We'll always need gifted, motivated case officers at the heart of the clandestine [secret] service. We'll always need good analysts to make a clean and clear picture out of the fragments of what our spies and satellites put on the table."[6] Techint provides the raw material, but human analysts provide the final objective: the finished intelligence.

Analyzing Secret
Intelligence:
Interpreting Images
and Cracking Codes

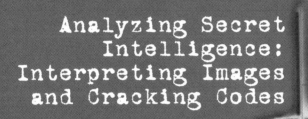

5

Here is what a landmark CIA intelligence report said about the Soviet Union:

> Soviet President Mikhail Gorbachev and other Soviet leaders are concerned about serious future breakdowns of public order in the USSR. This condition is well justified. The unrest that has punctuated Gorbachev's rule is not a transient [temporary] phenomenon. Conditions are likely to lead in the foreseeable future to continuing crises and instability on an even larger scale—in the form of mass demonstrations, strikes, violence, and perhaps even the localized emergence of parallel centers of power.[1]

This intelligence report, which foresees the breakup of the Soviet Union, was written in the late 1980s, a few years before the Soviet Union's actual breakup. In 1991, the Soviet Union split into 15 separate, independent republics, and America's enemy for nearly half a century suddenly ceased to exist.

Intelligence expert Jeffrey Richelson says, "I think they [the CIA] did a good job. If you had read the estimates and studies that I read from 1985 to May of 1991, I don't think anybody would have been surprised by the evolution of events in the Soviet Union, and that's all that anybody could ask."[2]

By "all that anybody could ask," Richelson means that CIA intelligence analysts produced long-range intelligence forecasts that did what they were designed to do: identify present trends—describe what was happening at the moment—and speculate on where those trends might lead in the future. The success of the CIA in analyzing Soviet intelligence was based on the effective use of the intelligence process, from start to finish.

THE INTELLIGENCE PROCESS

After intelligence has been gathered, experts analyze and evaluate the information, drawing conclusions and presenting those conclusions in a finished intelligence product to consumers.

Steps in the Intelligence Process

1. Intercept and collect intelligence.
2. Analyze and evaluate it.
3. Draw conclusions.
4. Present conclusions in an intelligence report.

When we think of consumers, we generally think of people who buy manufactured goods such as CDs, clothes, and cars. But in the intelligence community, *consumers* refers to key policymakers. These include the president and key members of Congress, who are responsible for running the government, and key military leaders.

ANALYZING IMINT

Analysts assemble their reports by gathering all the relevant material collected from satellite imagery, transcripts of intercepted telephone calls, e-mail messages, foreign government reports, newspaper stories, and other sources.

But before intelligence analysts can use this raw material, some of it must be converted. For example, the electro-optical signals collected by spy satellites must be turned into visible images, which is done by computers. Two more sets of experts must then see these images before they go to intelligence analysts.

First they go to photogrammetrists. The photogrammetrist's job is to determine the size and dimensions of objects that appear in these images. Photogrammetrists use the shadows cast by these objects, among other techniques, as clues to their size and dimensions. These images then go to imagery interpreters, who try to determine the identity of each object and the purpose that it serves.

The science known as crateology is a striking example of how imagery interpreters can produce vital intelligence. Crateology was developed during the Cold War years, when the Soviet Union was shipping vast quantities of military supplies to nations that were either part of the Soviet Union, behind the Iron Curtain, such as Poland and Czechoslovakia, or were supported by the Soviet Union, such as North Vietnam and Cuba.

Most of these Soviet military supplies, including tanks and fighter planes, were shipped by sea. To keep the contents of these shipments secret from America, the Soviets put everything into crates before bringing it out into the open for loading onto cargo vessels for shipment.

Crateology was used to identify the contents of these crates on board a Soviet ship. Once exposed, intelligence officers had visual confirmation that the crates contained airplane fuselages that the Soviets were bringing to Cuba during the Cuban Missile Crisis.

U.S. spy planes and satellites photographed these crates. Working with the resulting images, photogrammetrists and imagery interpreters devised a system for identifying the contents of Soviet arms shipments, depending on the size and shape of the crates. For example, they determined that crates of one certain size and shape were always used to transport Soviet jet fighter planes, MIG-29s. Thanks to crateology, the U.S. military was able to track many Soviet shipments of fighter planes, as well as other weapons, based on the size and shape of the crates being loaded onto or unloaded from Soviet cargo vessels.

Crateology was effective, but not foolproof. Once the Soviets discovered what U.S. intelligence was doing, they began using different shapes and sizes of crates to confuse U.S. photogrammetrists and imagery interpreters—all part of the continuing Cold War era sparring between the two superpowers.

EARLY USE OF CODES

Like satellite imagery, some Comint must be converted before intelligence analysts can use it. Foreign-language intelligence must be translated into English, and coded intelligence must be decoded.

The first known use of codes to transmit secret intelligence was by the Spartans in the 5th century B.C. in their wars against other Greeks. The Spartans wrapped a narrow strip of leather or parchment tightly around a long staff of a certain precise diameter, then wrote the secret message along the length of the staff. They then unwound this strip and rolled it up for transport. The receiver of the message unwound the strip and wound it back around another staff of the same exact diameter as the staff used to write it. Only then would the letters and numbers in the message line up to make sense. This code became known as the Skytale of the Spartans.

Breaking codes is the work of cryptanalysts. William Montgomery was a cryptanalyst whose work changed history.

During World War I, Montgomery, an Englishman, worked on breaking secret codes used by Germany, England's enemy in the war. In January 1917, British intelligence intercepted a coded telegram from the German Foreign Secretary, Arthur Zimmermann, that was meant for the German Minister in Mexico. The telegram began:

130 13042 13401 8501 115 3528 416

The coded message continued in this way, with a series of three- and four-digit numbers. Montgomery managed to decode the Zimmermann telegram after several days. The message began:

> We intend to begin on the first of February unrestricted submarine warfare.[3]

The telegram went on to say that if America, which had not yet joined the war, decided to fight on the side of the British, Germany would like Mexico to join their side and invade America. The decoded telegram was sent to Washington and released to U.S. newspapers in March 1917. The Zimmermann Telegram sparked outrage against Germany throughout America, and one month later the United States declared war on Germany.

MODERN CODES AND CIPHERS

How are codes and ciphers different? In a cipher, each individual letter is replaced with another according to some consistent plan. Here is a message in cipher.

Hppe tqjft lopx ipx up lffq tfdsfut.

The message appears baffling at first glance, but once you break the cipher it's easy to figure out. The plan behind this particular cipher is simple: Replace each letter in the original message with the previous letter in the alphabet; so, *Hppe* reads *Good*, and so forth.

Messages in code, such as the Zimmermann Telegram, do not use a consistent plan to replace individual letters. Instead, individual words or phrases are replaced by groups of numbers or letters found opposite the word or phrase in a codebook. To crack the code, a cryptanalyst must first figure out the opponent's codebook. To accomplish this, the cryptanalyst examines a series of messages, looking for patterns. For example, since the letter *E* is the most commonly used letter in the English language, the most commonly used number in the coded messages might stand for *E*.

Through most of the Cold War years, NSA cryptanalysts worked to invent new codes and ciphers for American secret agencies and to break opponents' codes and ciphers. Hardly anyone outside the NSA worked on making and breaking secret codes. This situation began changing in the mid-1980s as more and more people outside the government began using personal computers. People who wrote program codes for personal computers began inventing secret codes and selling them commercially in the form of computer software products. This trend continued until, by the mid-1990s, instead of inventing their own codes and ciphers, NSA cryptanalysts were buying them right off the shelves of computer software stores.

UNCRACKABLE CODES

Throughout the 1990s and into the 21st century, these commercial products, known as encryption software, became more and more sophisticated. The most sophisticated of these encryption products, called private-key code systems, revolutionized cryptanalysis. In previous code systems, if you could figure out the opponent's codebook, you could break the code. But what if there was no codebook shared by the sender and receiver? What if the sender used one system to encode the message and the receiver used another system to decode it? What if the receiver was the only person on Earth with the means to decode the secret message?

Private-key cryptography revolutionized the science of sending and receiving secret messages. With private-key cryptography, only the receiver has access to the decoding software and secret decryption key that unlocks the sender's message. This means that anyone with a computer and the right software can produce a virtually unbreakable code.

This situation troubles secret agencies charged with maintaining national security. FBI director Louis Freeh said, "The looming spectre of the widespread use of robust, virtually uncrackable encryption is one of the most difficult problems confronting law enforcement. . . . Uncrackable encryption will allow drug lords, spies, terrorists, and even violent gangs to communicate about their crimes and their conspiracies with impunity [freely]."[4]

The Senate Select Committee on Intelligence (SSCI) agreed with Freeh. A report issued by the SSCI states that the NSA's ability to deal with the private-key encryption situation is in serious doubt.[5]

Besides making life difficult for cryptanalysts and law enforcement agencies, private-key encryption makes life harder for intelligence analysts. The more secret messages that remain secret, the less information the analyst has to work with.

AUTHENTICATING THE PUZZLE PIECES

Once the collected intelligence has been converted and examined for relevance, it must be double-checked for authenticity. Jack Davis, a CIA intelligence officer, advises analysts, "Be able to answer the question: 'How do you know you are not being deceived?'"[6]

Analysts know that an opponent will use denial and disinformation to deceive them. Denial is a matter of concealing or camouflaging secrets. Disinformation is a matter of sending out false intelligence. This can be done through double agents who operate paper mills, producing false documents. It can also be done through government-controlled newspapers, radio, and television. The Soviet Union ran a disinformation campaign during the Cold War designed to deceive the world about the true extent of its military power. Government-controlled newspapers released figures claiming that the Soviet Union spent only 2 to 3 percent of its gross national product on defense when the true figure, as it turned out, was closer to 33 percent.[7]

PIECING THE PUZZLE TOGETHER

When analysts finish evaluating each bit of intelligence for accuracy, they are left with pieces of a puzzle. Analysts then begin the mental work of piecing this puzzle together and drawing conclusions from the results.

It is the analyst's responsibility to avoid being taken by surprise by sudden shifts in political, military, or economic activities. For example, during the late 1980s, CIA intelligence analysts issued reports warning of the imminent breakup of the Soviet Union. As noted earlier, these warnings helped U.S. political, military, and economic leaders prepare for significant changes in world power structures.

One thing an analyst looks for are "indicators," unusual occurrences in the day-to-day activities of political leaders, military forces, or the business community. For example, if commercial radio and television broadcasts in a foreign nation are suddenly interrupted and military marches are played instead, the government of that nation may be in the process of a military takeover. If military vehicles are suddenly diverted from their regular routes and sent to unfamiliar destinations, a military conflict may be brewing. If key political leaders suddenly begin giving speeches criticizing a nation they were thought to be friendly with, a change in relations with that nation may be coming.

The analyst must use these indicators to draw conclusions when direct information is missing. Much of the time the analyst has only bits and pieces of information to go on and must fill in the holes by inference and deduction—educated guesses. The analyst's conclusions, when they are accurate, reveal the secret intentions of America's opponents to the president and other key decision makers.

KEEPING AN OPEN MIND

The mind of a modern intelligence analyst works something like the mind of a scientist. Both use the scientific method, advancing hypotheses and theories based on a methodical examination of the evidence.

And both strive to keep an open mind, to maintain a healthy level of doubt about their conclusions, testing them and, when necessary, changing them. Intelligence analysts are trained to state conclusions strongly, but also to state doubts just as strongly. They must be honest about their conclusions, which means that they cannot afford to be arrogant. Arrogance, a tendency to consistently underestimate others, leads to misjudgments and self-deception.

The way U.S. intelligence analysts handled the Chernobyl disaster is an example of how arrogance can cloud thinking. On a Sunday evening in April 1986, operators of the Chernobyl nuclear reactor, located near the city of Kiev in the Soviet Union, ran an unauthorized experiment that caused a catastrophic explosion, killing hundreds and releasing massive doses of deadly radioactivity. The Soviet Union attempted to keep this catastrophe secret.

On Monday afternoon, officials in Sweden, some 800 miles (1,300 kilometers) north, reported that their air monitors were suddenly registering higher-than-normal traces of radioactivity. When U.S. intelligence analysts received the news about rising radiation levels from Sweden, they decided to disregard it. After all, they thought, the Swedes were always making a fuss about their air quality, registering major complaints over the tiniest amounts of radiation. The Swedes were just making a great big fuss over nothing, as usual, they thought.

The Soviets failed to keep the explosion secret for long. The next day, Tuesday, the whole world knew the truth of the catastrophe at Chernobyl, and U.S. intelligence analysts were embarrassed at what they'd done—or hadn't done. It was their duty to follow up on the Swedish complaint and investigate the causes of the higher-than-normal radiation readings, then issue an immediate warning of a nuclear crisis. But the analysts' arrogant underestimation of the Swedes kept them from seeing the truth. Besides making sure they are not being deceived by an opponent, intelligence analysts must make sure that they are not deceiving themselves.

Reporting Secret
Intelligence

6

A young economic analyst named Walter Levy was assigned to U.S. intelligence during World War II. Allied forces from America, Britain, and France were fighting the Axis forces from Germany, Italy, and Japan. Levy was given the difficult task of locating German oil refineries as potential targets for bombing. These refineries provided gasoline and motor oil for Germany's war machinery, and knocking out oil refineries would deal a crippling blow to the Allies' enemy.

The locations of these refineries were closely guarded secrets, and no U.S. spies or aerial reconnaissance planes had been able to find them. But being an economist, Levy knew of another intelligence source that no one else had thought of. He was able to collect this vital intelligence all by himself. He didn't need spy planes and he didn't need secret agents. All he had to do was look up public records. Levy knew that the German railroads published tax records of all shipments of gasoline and oil products. Using only these public shipment records, Levy was able to figure out the exact locations of the German refineries and report them to Allied forces for targeting.

OPEN SOURCE INTELLIGENCE

Intelligence gathered by spies (Humint) and by secret technical devices such as spy satellites and bugs (Techint) make up about 20 percent of the intelligence gathered for intelligence reports. The remaining 80 percent is open source intelligence—*Osint*, information that is available to anyone who seeks it.

Osint sources include information generated by media, such as newspaper stories and radio and television broadcasts, and technical papers published in journals and on the Internet. They include public reference sources such as maps, telephone books, and train schedules, and government information, such as census data, agricultural forecasts, and railroad shipment records, like those that Walter Levy used.

Osint is especially useful in tracking changing political trends around the world. What is happening in the government of an opponent nation? What is the state of health of its leader? How strong is the opposition to this leader? Are there any plans in place for a civil war? For a military overthrow of the government? For a presidential assassination? By keeping a close watch on open sources, intelligence agencies can answer questions like these.

Osint sources are not secret, and they are not closely guarded. Yet these sources can yield precious information to someone like Walter Levy, who knows how to make use of them.

WRITING INTELLIGENCE REPORTS

Some intelligence reports present a brief, up-to-the-minute summary of current world events as they relate to U.S. national security, without going into much detail on any one event. Others are lengthy and deal with a single event in depth. Some intelligence reports deal with sudden critical happenings, such as a terrorist attack, that may call for immediate action on the part of decision makers. Others are designed to keep decision makers informed about ongoing world situations that affect national security, such as the state of the world's oil supply.

But all intelligence reports are written to certain standards, which have been spelled out in a CIA training manual for intelligence analysts.[1] Here are a few of the standards, followed by brief explanations.

- "We interpret, not describe." Intelligence reports offer insight, not just facts.

- "We do not pile up detail. Data dumps are not the way to show our expertise." Only a small fraction of the raw information collected actually appears in an intelligence report.

- "We evaluate raw information critically to determine its relevance, reliability, and weight as evidence." Nothing is taken at face value. The information in an intelligence report has been carefully checked out.

- "We synthesize. We render the complex simple." An intelligence report is dominated by a few key ideas, each of which has been assembled from a great many smaller details.

- "We tell our consumers what is *really* happening in a situation." An intelligence report recognizes that we live in a world where things are not always what they seem.

- "We draw conclusions that are greater than the data they're based on." Intelligence reports look beyond the facts to what the facts point to, to what they suggest. They anticipate future trends and developments.

- "We have to make judgments on the basis of information that is incomplete, conflicting, and of varying degrees of reliability." An intelligence report is not the complete story. It is an attempt to come as close as possible to the truth of matters that can never be completely known or understood.

- "We need to provide the best possible answer given the time and information available." The best an intelligence report can do is give an accurate assessment of how things look at the moment, knowing that information is incomplete and that situations will change.

UP-TO-THE-MINUTE INTELLIGENCE REPORTS

The explosion of Techint from spy satellites has provided intelligence analysts with far more information than they can deal with. Intelligence consumers are in a similar dilemma. In one year alone, 1994, the CIA published some 35,000 intelligence reports. The CIA intelligence writers' manual refers to the modern intelligence consumer as "a busy reader who literally is 'in a hurry to stop reading.'"[2]

For this reason, intelligence consumers now favor short, summary-style reports over long, detailed analyses. The most prominent of these summary-style products is a top-secret report from the CIA known as the *President's Daily Briefing* (PDB). Every morning the President and twelve of his closest advisers receive it.

The PDB reports what is happening within the inner circles of power in key nations around the world. It always appears in written form, but some presidents have had it delivered in other forms as well. President Ronald Reagan viewed the PDB on videotape. Others have had the report read to them. This oral briefing is delivered in person by an intelligence officer. These face-to-face briefings give the President the chance to respond directly to PDB contents and get the officer's immediate feedback.

LONG-TERM INTELLIGENCE REPORTS

The analysts who produce current, up-to-the minute intelligence, such as the PDB, are known as "butchers." They must do their work quickly in order to keep it fresh. They do not have the luxury of time. The analysts who produce long-term intelligence reports are known as "bakers." They can take more time and care with their work, refining it to get more thoughtful results.

The bakers are responsible for long-term intelligence reports called *National Intelligence Estimates* (NIEs). These reports look at the directions that a major issue or trend has taken over the last several years and at the directions in which it appears to be heading. They typically focus on a particular foreign country, political leader, or world problem, such as controlling the spread of nuclear weapons.

NIEs can take anywhere from a few months to a year or more to create. They are said to represent the considered opinion of the entire intelligence community. NIEs are seen as the best products that intelligence has to offer. They are thoroughly and thoughtfully researched and prepared.

But that doesn't mean that everyone who reads an NIE agrees with what it says. In fact, NIEs traditionally generate controversy and, sometimes, full-scale debate that reaches the highest levels of government.

A CONTROVERSIAL REPORT

A 1999 National Intelligence Estimate (NIE) on the threat posed by rogue nations that have intercontinental ballistic missile (ICBM) bases led to high-level controversy and debate. Rogue nations are nations known for their aggressive and sometimes unpredictable behavior toward neighboring nations and the United States. These rogue nations include Cuba, Iran, Iraq, Libya, North Korea, Sudan, and Syria. The 1999 NIE was written because President Bill Clinton and members of Congress were debating whether to budget $60 billion to build a national missile defense system (NMD) to protect the United

This timed exposure shows a test run of the U.S. Peacekeeper intercontinental ballistic missiles, headed through the clouds to an open ocean impact zone.

States against this rogue nation threat. "Next year," Clinton said in June 1999, "we will, for the first time, determine whether to deploy a limited National Missile Defense, when we review the results of flight tests and other developmental efforts, consider cost estimates and evaluate the threat."[3]

Was there a real threat from these rogue nations? And if so, how great a threat was it? The 1999 NIE concluded that "during the next 15 years the United States most likely will face ICBM threats from Russia, China, and North Korea, probably from Iran, and possibly from Iraq."[4] But among these nations, the report concluded, North Korea, with its Rodong missile base, posed the most likely threat (see Chapter 3, "Spies in the Sky").

Critics of the national missile defense system called the NIE report unnecessarily alarming. The report failed to mention diplomatic efforts to improve United States–North Korea relations, which, they said, could eventually lead to an easing of tensions between the two nations.

Critics also noted that the report based the so-called threat on the fact that North Korea "could" continue testing missiles, not that it was "likely" to do any further testing, and there was a world of difference between being able to do something and being likely to do it. This narrow but crucial difference in language unfairly pushed the report toward favoring a worst-case scenario, critics said.

On the other side, supporters of the national missile defense system saw the 1999 NIE as insightful and realistic. They pointed out that the world had changed drastically with the breakup of the Soviet Union in 1991. During the Cold War years, between 1945 and 1991, the United States and the Soviet Union had an unspoken understanding. Neither side would start a nuclear war, knowing that their equally powerful opponent would retaliate, and that the results would be catastrophic for everyone. Both superpowers understood that there could be no winner in a nuclear war between them. This understanding was known as "mutual deterrence."

Mutual deterrence was a key element of the Cold War mindset. But times had changed, and mindsets had changed with the times. So-called rogue nations sometimes took reckless actions, such as Iraq's invasion of Kuwait in 1990, that were not necessarily for the rogue nation's own good. Leon S. Fuerth, a national security adviser in the Clinton administration, said, "We did not like the Soviets, but we roughly understood them to be extremely cautious. We never had the depth of understanding about what makes the North Koreans tick to give us that confidence."[5]

The 1999 NIE helped fuel the controversy over the national missile defense system. Problems encountered in testing the system added to the problem. The issue finally became so controversial that President Clinton elected to set it aside and leave it for the next administration to resolve. In a speech delivered on September 1, 2000, Clinton said that the United States "should not move forward until we have absolute confidence the system will work."[6]

Intelligence reports sometimes influence government policy decisions. Clinton based his decision to abandon the NMD proposal at least partly on the fact that it had not received the kind of support it would need to pass a vote in Congress. Reaction to the controversial NIE report helped make this fact clear.

Clinton left office in January 2001. The new President, George W. Bush, quickly took up the national missile defense issue. Bush decided to pursue the program despite the fact that the rogue nation posing the most likely threat, North Korea, had backed off from missile testing. In May 2001, North Korea pledged to put an end to the tests until 2003. North Korean leader Kim Jong II suggested that this pledge would be extended if the Bush administration showed a willingness to pursue better relations with North Korea. But President Bush insisted that "We need a new framework that allows us to build missile defenses to counter the different threats of today's world."[7]

Using Secret
Intelligence:
Successes
and Failures

7

Success and failure in the world of intelli-gence and espionage are always paired. Success for one side means failure for the other. Two incidents from World War II, Pearl Harbor and the Battle of Midway, serve as examples.

On December 7, 1941, Japanese military forces attacked the American Pacific Fleet, which was based in and around Pearl Harbor, on the island of Oahu in Hawaii. The United States had not yet officially joined the war, and the attack on U.S. forces was a complete surprise. The United States suf-fered heavy casualties, and much of the Pacific Fleet was destroyed. As a result of the Pearl Harbor sneak attack, the United States entered the war against Japan and Germany at less than full strength.

Naval Captain Joseph J. Rochefort was in charge of intel-ligence at Pearl Harbor. He said that the main reason U.S. forces were caught off guard was their failure to break the Japanese code. The Japanese military had started using a new code just six days earlier, and U.S. cryptanalysts had not yet managed to break it. If U.S. secret intelligence had been able to intercept Japanese messages during those six days, U.S.

forces might have known about the Pearl Harbor attack in advance. An intelligence success for Japan meant an intelligence failure for the United States.

Six months later, fortunes were reversed, and once again intelligence played a significant role. U.S. cryptanalysts had cracked Japan's naval code and learned that Japan was about to invade the U.S.–held island of Midway, at the westernmost tip of the Hawaiian chain. U.S. naval forces were still not at full strength. This intelligence breakthrough allowed them to catch the attacking Japanese by surprise and defeat Japan's superior fleet during the three-day Battle of Midway in June 1942. This time an intelligence success for the United States meant an intelligence failure for Japan.

SUCCESSES AND FAILURES

We know that secrecy is a key element in the world of espionage, and we know that is what makes this world seem intriguing and mysterious. But it also keeps much of this world concealed from view. A great many happenings in the world of spies and spying remain hidden from the public. This is especially true of success stories. Since secret agencies want their opponents to know as little as possible about what they do and how they do it, they seldom publicize their successes.

Keeping success a secret is not difficult. When it comes to intelligence and espionage, success is usually a nonevent. It means that something bad *didn't* happen. Failures, on the other hand, are hard to keep secret, and the greater the failure the harder it is to hide. Mistakes by secret agencies make for news headlines, which are often followed by highly publicized congressional investigations, which generally lead to criticism of the secret agencies involved.

So when it comes to the use of intelligence and espionage, many more failures come to light than successes, and this tends to reflect badly on the work of the intelligence community. This is especially true in modern times. Decades from now more success stories will come to light. For now, we know far more about the failures of modern secret agencies than their successes. We need to keep this in mind as we examine two highly publicized events that show what can go wrong when secret agencies fail to follow their own strict rules.

THE CHINESE EMBASSY BOMBING

On May 7, 1999, a U.S. B-2 bomber was headed for Belgrade, the capital of Yugoslavia. The bomber carried five 2000-pound Joint Direct Attack Munitions, satellite-guided "smart" weapons. U.S. forces were in Yugoslavia to help bring an end to the bloody conflict between warring ethnic forces of Serbs and Muslims. The Yugoslav regime was largely responsible for the bloodshed. The Yugoslav Federal Directorate of Supply and Procurement (FDSP) headquarters was the major source of Yugoslav currency. By destroying it, U.S. forces hoped to bring chaos to the Yugoslav economy and to slow, perhaps even stop, the Yugoslav regime's war efforts. Intelligence sources had told the B-2 bomber's crew that the FDSP was located at Bulevar Umetnosti 2 in New Belgrade, so that was where the crew dropped their bombs.

The five bombs hit their target squarely—but they also missed it. The building at Bulevar Umetnosti 2 was destroyed, but this building was not the FDSP. It was the Chinese Embassy. Three Chinese civilians were killed in the tragic bombing, and twenty others were wounded. The accidental bombing of the Chinese Embassy in Belgrade was a classic case of the misuse of open-source intelligence.

WHAT WENT WRONG

The agency responsible for supplying the intelligence for the FDSP bombing mission was the National Imagery and Mapping Agency (NIMA). NIMA describes itself as the intelligence agency that "provides timely, relevant, and accurate imagery, imagery intelligence, and geospatial [satellite] information in support of military, national-level, and civil users."[1]

The accidental bombing of the Chinese Embassy in Belgrade was an intelligence failure with costs measured in human lives, in addition to being a diplomatic disaster.

In other words, NIMA is responsible for supplying up-to-date maps and satellite imagery for intelligence use. Under Secretary of State Thomas Pickering, who presented a State Department report on the tragedy, said that "multiple factors and errors in several parts of the U.S. Government were responsible for the mistaken bombing."[2]

But NIMA bore the lion's share of responsibility. It was NIMA officials who provided the maps that the pilots used to locate their target, and those maps were fatally out of date. But even with NIMA's outdated maps, the tragedy should never have happened. The CIA was responsible for verifying the FDSP location. U.S. officials who had lived in Belgrade and knew the city could have been consulted. If CIA officials had shown them the outdated maps, they would have seen that the wrong address had been targeted, but this never happened.

The CIA had also ordered satellite images of the building at Bulevar Umetnosti 2. The FDSP was a squared-off building, but the Chinese Embassy looked something like a pagoda, with curved edges and a narrow peak. If CIA officials had examined these images closely, they would have seen that the targeted building could not possibly have been the FDSP, but they never did this.

No blame fell on the flight crew who dropped the bombs. They were at too high an altitude to be able to notice the distinctive Chinese architecture of the building. When Under Secretary of State Pickering said, "No one, at any stage in the process, realized that our bombs were aimed at the Chinese Embassy," he was right in two ways.[3] The bombing was entirely unintentional, and the bombing should never have happened.

Osint figured prominently in this tragedy. These public-intelligence sources can be used to discover a person's age and place of birth and hair color and eye color. They can provide a person's telephone number and e-mail address. They can reveal a person's home address and the addresses where businesses and government agencies are housed. Osint sources can give a profile of each and every street in a city and of the people who live there and how to reach them.

But this profile keeps changing. Addresses change as people, businesses, and government agencies move to new locations. The accidental bombing of the Chinese Embassy in Belgrade never would have happened if intelligence agencies had followed their own rules and kept their public sources on the city of Belgrade up to date.

INDIAN NUCLEAR TESTS

During the Cold War years, only two nations, the United States and the Soviet Union, had nuclear weapons. By the beginning of the 21st century that number had grown to perhaps as many as ten nations. A 1999 report to the U.S. Congress stated that nuclear proliferation, the spread of nuclear weapons, posed "a grave threat to the United States, to our military forces, and our vital interests abroad." The report called for "a new strategy focused not just on prevention, but also on combating all aspects of proliferation."[4]

Nearly all the nations of the world publicly agreed that nuclear proliferation represented a dire threat not only to world peace but to all human life on the planet. But privately, some nations were suspected of developing nuclear weapons, and these nations were being watched by U.S. secret agencies. The neighboring nations of Pakistan and India, who had been threatening each other for decades, were on the list of nations to watch. In 1995, U.S. spy satellites sent back images of equipment being moved around at India's nuclear test site at Pokharan, southwest of the capital city of New Delhi.

U.S. Ambassador to India Frank Wisner, Jr., showed these images to top Indian officials and tried to persuade them to change their plans. Together, the spy satellite images and Wisner's diplomatic persuasion worked as intended. India agreed not to test nuclear weapons. The result represented a triumph of diplomacy and top-flight intelligence work.

WHAT WENT WRONG

U.S. intelligence agencies continued to watch, but now India was watching too. India had a space program of its own. As part of this program, Indian engineers and scientists had developed the technology to track satellites' orbits, and they used this technology to keep a constant eye on U.S. spy satellites. This time the Indians were careful to move equipment around at the Pokharan site only when these spies in the sky weren't watching. In this way, India continued to secretly develop nuclear weapons.

By 1998, U.S. policy makers and intelligence officials had reached a consensus opinion that India was no longer a threat to test nuclear weapons. Then two events challenged that opinion. First, in March 1998, a new political party, the Bharatiya Janta Party, came to power, and party officials pledged that the government would begin testing nuclear weapons. Then, in April, India's neighbor and enemy, Pakistan, tested a new ballistic missile capable of reaching major Indian cities.

But U.S. policy makers and intelligence officials continued to believe that India had no intentions of testing nuclear weapons. Then, on May 8, 1998, satellite images showed renewed activity at the Pokharan test site. But these images escaped the notice of CIA intelligence analysts responsible for tracking the Indian nuclear program. One reason was the prevailing opinion that India was not going to test; another was the huge volume of spy satellite images the analysts had to look through every day.

One CIA analyst did notice an image showing fences being removed at the site, but by the time his warning reached higher-ranking officers, it was too late. India had already exploded a nuclear bomb, on May 11, 1998, just as their ruling party had promised. The result was a growing nuclear arms race between India and its rival, Pakistan.

In intelligence circles, "mirror imaging" is a state of mind that analysts are warned to avoid. Mirror imaging means assuming that another person will behave a certain way simply because you would behave that way. Mirror imaging is the failure to account for the "otherness" of your opponent, the many ways that your opponent differs from you. U.S. intelligence officials had decided that after their 1995 triumph of intelligence and diplomacy, India was now firmly on the side of nuclear nonproliferation. They failed to account for the combination of national pride and worry about Pakistan that drove India to show the world that they were a force to be reckoned with.

The Chinese Embassy bombing and the Indian nuclear test show errors of judgment that would never have been made if intelligence officers and analysts had followed the rules of their trade to the letter. "The attack [on the Chinese Embassy] was a mistake," said Under Secretary of State Thomas Pickering, "a series of errors and omissions."[5]

"Look, we were wrong," said Phyllis Oakley, the State Department's highest-ranking intelligence officer, at a Senate hearing on the Indian nuclear test. "We were all wrong."[6]

ONE MORE FAILURE

On September 11, 2001, terrorists piloted hijacked commercial airliners into New York's World Trade Center and the Pentagon in Washington, D.C., killing thousands. Terrorists living in U.S. cities had been planning the attacks for months. But U.S. intelligence had no warning of the method, timing, or location of the attacks.

This intelligence failure drew sharp criticism from several sources, including the intelligence community itself. The chairman of the Senate Select Committee on Intelligence, Senator Bob Graham, said that the failure showed a serious lack of coordination among U.S. intelligence services. Graham promised that Senate hearings would be held to determine exactly what went wrong and why.

Industrial
Espionage

8

On a May morning in 1991, a man stands guard at a large home in a wealthy Houston, Texas, suburb. The owner of the home is a defense contractor with the U.S. government. He deals in materials for the manufacture of weapons and defense systems such as airplanes, tanks, and satellites. The guard notices some peculiar activity in the alley in back of the house. Two well-dressed men are rummaging through the owner's trash cans and stuffing the trash into plastic bags. The guard watches as they tie up the bags, throw them into a van, and drive off.

The guard copies down the van's license plate number. The number is reported to the FBI. The FBI traces the van to the office of Bernard Guillet, the French consul general in Houston. When Guillet is questioned by FBI agents, he admits that he and an assistant were the two well-dressed men in the alley that morning. They were there, Guillet said, because of the hole in his back yard. He'd had the hole dug for a swimming pool, but due to a zoning dispute, the pool could not be built, so now he had a big hole to fill. Guillet wasn't collecting the defense contractor's trash that morning, he claimed. He and his assistant were just gathering grass clippings to help fill the swimming pool hole.

The French consul general was being less than truthful. He and his assistant were engaging in a well-known method of espionage. Examining an opponent's trash has become such a common intelligence-gathering method, especially for industrial espionage, that the intelligence community has given it an official name. That May morning the consul general and his assistant were engaged in the espionage technique known as *Trashint*.

EARLY USES OF INDUSTRIAL ESPIONAGE

Industrial espionage is the collecting of business intelligence by illegal means, usually by a competitor or an intelligence agency. Industrial espionage can be a matter of a foreign nation spying on U.S. businesses, one U.S. business spying on another, or an unhappy employee walking out with a computer disk full of trade secrets to sell to a rival.

Like other forms of espionage, industrial espionage began long ago. In the sixth century A.D., Justinian, emperor of the Eastern Roman Empire, sent monks to China as his envoys. These Roman envoys were supposed to be friendly representatives of Justinian's government, but they were really spies sent to steal trade secrets. The Chinese had developed an elegant and expensive fabric called silk, which only they knew how to produce. The Chinese had jealously guarded the secrets of silk production for some 30 centuries. But Justinian's envoys soon discovered the secret—silkworms. They managed to smuggle the secret back to Europe by collecting silk-moth eggs and concealing them in the hollowed-out ends of their walking sticks. Later, when the eggs hatched, silkworm larvae emerged, and Europe had solved the ancient Chinese mystery of silk-making.

Perhaps one of the greatest feats of industrial espionage in history was accomplished in 1811 by a spy with an astonishing memory. Francis Cabot Lowell, a skilled mathematician from Boston, Massachusetts, journeyed to Scotland. Lowell claimed he'd come for his health, but that was his cover story. His real reason was to steal secrets. England and Scotland had amazing machines called water-driven looms. A single loom in Scotland or England could turn out more cloth than a thousand skilled laborers in America.

Britain and Scotland had a monopoly on the looms that had made them rich. Americans before Lowell had tried everything to figure out how the looms worked, without success. Walls surrounding the mills were topped with glass shards and spikes. The looms were guarded day and night. No one was allowed to examine them closely or draw any pictures.

Foreigners were allowed to tour the mills, though, and look at the looms. The owners assumed that the machines were too complex for anyone to understand by just looking. They didn't know about Lowell's brilliant memory. After touring a Scottish mill, he came away with enough information in his head to actually draw up the plans for a water-driven loom on paper. Back in Boston, Lowell and a mechanic managed to build a working replica from these plans, and Lowell soon had mills in America producing up to 30 miles (48 kilometers) of cloth a day.

INDUSTRIAL ESPIONAGE METHODS

Industrial spies try to gain as much information as possible from their target's confidential files without getting compromised. Like their historical predecessors, modern industrial spies are inventive. But with the added advantages of modern technologies, they have many more tools to work with. FBI director Louis Freeh said that "practitioners of economic espionage seldom use one collection method in isolation. Rather, they conduct well-orchestrated programs that combine both legal and illegal, traditional and more innovative methods."[1]

Computer Espionage

With modern electronic communications, many businesses have become more efficient and more profitable, but also more vulnerable to industrial espionage. Every new communications pathway is another potential point of entry for spies. And the more efficient that pathway, the more potentially valuable it is for industrial spies.

Computer networks are one of those pathways. E-mail messages can be intercepted by hackers, and computer files can be downloaded. By copying a single computer hard drive, a modern industrial spy could conceivably gather enough information in a few minutes to make millions of dollars for a competitor.

In March 1999 the federal government announced that it had fired Wen Ho Lee, a nuclear scientist at the Los Alamos National Laboratory in New Mexico, for "serious security violations" involving computer espionage. Lee was accused of copying huge amounts of information about the U.S. nuclear weapons program from government computers, including secret data about America's most advanced nuclear warhead, the W-88. Lee, a Chinese-American, was also suspected of selling this secret information to China, which could encourage China to accelerate its nuclear weapons program.

In September 2000, the government reduced its 59-count indictment against him to a single count of mishandling classified information and failing to report contacts with Chinese scientists. Lee confessed to the one count, but he did not confess to giving any classified information to China. Lee was released from custody, having already served nine months in solitary confinement.

Electronic Eavesdropping

Telephones are another pathway open to the industrial spy. Wiretapping is the interception of a telephone conversation by accessing the telephone signal. Wiretapping is legal only if

A listening device that fits neatly into most
telephones. These devices are sold at retail
spy stores across the country.

done by a law enforcement agency and authorized by the court. A device known as a "slave unit" is the telephone tap most widely used by both law enforcement officers and spies. The unit, housed in a small plastic box, is installed like a bridge across two telephone lines located near each other. One is the target's line; the other is the spy's. When a call comes over the target line, the slave silently bridges the two lines, sending the call through the spy's line as well as the caller's.

Phone taps are almost impossible to detect; a tapped phone does not click or buzz. Devices known as "pen registers" can be attached to a phone line to record the telephone numbers of incoming calls, while "trap and trace devices" record the numbers of outgoing calls.

Industrial spies also use bugs and radio scanners for electronic eavesdropping. Bugs concealed in hard-to-find places can monitor live conversations (see Chapter 2, "Listening Devices"). Radio scanners can monitor cordless and cellular phone conversations.

The Phantom Interview

There are two varieties of phantom interviews. In both, the spy is an impostor. In the first, the spy poses as an employment recruiter for a competitor trying to lure employees away from a competing company to his company by claiming to offer a better position at higher pay. During the interview, the spy asks questions about the employee's present duties and responsibilities, hoping to gain inside information on the competitor's operations.

In the second variety, the positions are reversed. The spy comes to the competitor for a job interview. Posing as a job seeker, the spy asks questions about how the business is run, hoping to gain inside information.

The Insider

An insider is a trusted person inside the competing company with access to valuable information. Ira Winkler, a security consultant who advises corporations on preventing industrial espionage, wrote: "These people [insiders] know how to hurt you. They know your prized secrets, they know your competitors, and they usually know how to hide their actions. What is perhaps most damaging about insider espionage is that it goes unnoticed. Your competitors are beating you to the punch, you're losing market share, and no one knows why."[2]

Dr. Ronald Hoffman was an insider who did a great deal of damage. Hoffman was a rocket scientist and lead researcher for Science Applications International Corporation (SAIC). Between 1986 and 1990 Hoffman secretly copied technical data on space technology developed by SAIC for the U.S. Air Force and sold it to four Japanese companies for a reported $700,000. According to press reports, the information helped these four Japanese companies gain significant ground in their own development of space technology. In April 1992, Hoffman was convicted of industrial espionage, sentenced to two years in prison, and fined $225,000.

Theft
Within the United States, there is a cash market for information such as a company's customer lists, financial records, and expansion plans. This information is sometimes obtained by breaking and entering. Overseas, the theft of laptop computers has become a common way of stealing company secrets. Ghislain Levesque, an economic espionage investigator who advises executives on how to avoid industrial spies overseas, said, "I always say in my presentations that before taking a foreign trip, executives must do a mental check of what's on their laptop hard drive; they should take only the information that is absolutely necessary. Don't take your entire company in your laptop; you may lose it all."[3]

Misinformation Campaigns
Spreading misinformation is a particularly effective way of gaining an economic advantage over a competitor. This method of industrial espionage involves spreading a series of

damaging lies about a competitor, using the mass media. Here is an example: During the early 1990s a film screened throughout Japan showed pictures of deformed babies. This film claimed, falsely, that the babies' injuries had come from eating food products exported to Japan from the United States. The film was sponsored by the Japanese government in cooperation with Japanese business groups. They used the film to persuade Japanese citizens not to buy American baby food. The Japanese government has a long record of making it difficult for American businesses to export food products for sale in Japan.

Hiring Detectives

Corporations sometimes hire private detectives to do their industrial spying. These detectives follow rivals and go through their trash. Sometimes they manage to get themselves hired. As employees, they then take advantage of opportunities to steal information from inside the competitor's offices. Detectives also attend conventions and trade shows where competitors set up booths to show off their latest product models and technological innovations. The FBI estimates that one in fifty people at any given trade show is there to gather intelligence for a competitor.

Touring Plants

During the Cold War years the Soviet Union mounted a sophisticated campaign of economic espionage in the United States, spending over a billion dollars a year in salaries and bribes to steal details about U.S. weapons systems. Despite being fierce rivals during the Cold War, America and the Soviet Union made friendly gestures toward each other from time to time. One of these gestures was taking selected visitors on tours. In 1983 a Soviet delegation of scientists toured the Grumman Aircraft plant on Long Island, in New York. The Soviets could carry no cameras and take no notes of any kind. But they still managed to bring valuable information out with them by putting adhesive tape on their shoes. On the tape they collected slivers of metal alloys from the floor of the plant to take back to the Soviet Union. The metal slivers were made of secret alloys used in the manufacture of new U.S. fighter planes.

PREVENTING INDUSTRIAL ESPIONAGE

Since the end of the Cold War, incidents of industrial espionage have increased. In a 1992 report to the Senate, Secretary of Defense William Cohen said, "Our competitors—even our closest allies—do not always play by the rules. Indicative of this is the alarming rate at which foreign governments are spying on U.S. businesses and economic interests."[4]

Typical targets include scientists traveling abroad, especially in Pakistan, China, and Russia. According to congressional investigators, these scientists have been targeted by foreign agents, who bug their hotel rooms, rifle through their suitcases, and steal their briefcases and laptop computers.

To respond to this surge in industrial espionage, the U.S. Congress passed the Economic Espionage Act of 1996. The law states, "Typically espionage has focused on military secrets. But as the Cold War has drawn to a close, this classic form of espionage has evolved. Economic superiority is increasingly as important as military superiority. And the espionage industry is being retooled with this in mind."[5]

With the passage of this legislation, industrial espionage became a federal crime. Penalties for violators were stiffened, and the FBI joined the fight against them. Preventive measures include helping to keep U.S. business executives from becoming targets of industrial spies while traveling overseas. The FBI and CIA work together to gather intelligence and inform specific companies that they have been targeted by foreign agents.

The FBI works to track down industrial spies within U.S. borders. One domestic spy was an engineer named Steven L.

Davis. Davis was employed by an engineering firm that helped develop a new shaving system for the Gillette company, headquartered in Boston, Massachusetts. Davis was angry at his supervisor and fearful that he was about to lose his job. He was a disgruntled employee.

Security consultant Ira Winkler tells business executives that disgruntled employees pose a real threat to their organizations. "It's usually not about money for these folks; what they want is to feel important. And that makes them dangerous. Disgruntled employees are easily manipulated by outsiders and are considered an important resource among professional spies."[6]

Davis got back at his company by stealing their secrets. In March 1997, he stole trade secrets concerning the design of Gillette's new shaving system and gave them to three of Gillette's leading competitors, Warner-Lambert Company, American Safety Razor Company, and Bic. Davis was convicted of espionage and sentenced to 27 months in prison and more than one million dollars in fines. At his sentencing hearing, Davis confessed that he engaged in this espionage to hurt his employer and supervisor, and did not do it for the money.

According to the FBI, industrial espionage against U.S. companies is on the rise. A survey estimated that losses from foreign and domestic espionage exceeded $300 billion in 1998 alone.[7] Pierre Marion, former head of the French intelligence service, which has spied on U.S. companies for the benefit of French companies, said, "It would not be normal that we spy on the United States in political matters or in military matters. We are allied, but in the economic competition, in the technological competition, we are competitors. We are not allied."[8]

Counterintelligence and
Counterespionage

9

Intelligence is about stealing an opponent's vital information. Counterintelligence is about concealing your own vital information from your opponent. The first task of counterintelligence is deciding what information is important enough to protect. Protected information is labeled as classified. There are three kinds of classified information, based on the degree of damage that each kind of information could do if it were to fall into enemy hands.

The more secret the information, the fewer members of an intelligence agency are cleared—allowed—to see it. That way, secret information has a smaller chance of reaching the enemy. This process is known as compartmentation: putting classified information into separate "compartments" to which only certain selected individuals have access.

To access Top Secret information, an intelligence employee must have special clearance. But that is not all. The employee must also have "a need to know." An employee may see certain information, such as secret documents and photographs, only if that information directly concerns an assignment the employee is working on at the time. For example, if

Type of Classified Information	Degree of Damage
Top Secret	Exceptionally serious damage
Secret	Serious damage
Confidential	Damage

you were a cryptanalyst decoding secret e-mail messages passed between narcotics traffickers, you would not have access to Top Secret information on nuclear weapons technology. This is how the information security system is designed to work. However, as we shall see, the system does not always work as designed.

COUNTERINTELLIGENCE AT WORK

The FBI is in charge of counterintelligence operations. It is its responsibility to see that foreign intelligence agents operating in America do not steal government secrets. The FBI defines its mission as "detecting and counteracting foreign intelligence activity that gathers information that adversely affects U.S. national interests or security."[1]

To do this detecting and counteracting, the FBI uses sophisticated technology and shrewd detective work. They used a combination of both to apprehend Stanislav Gusev, the Russian intelligence officer operating under cover of being Second Secretary in the Russian Embassy (see Introduction).

Eventually, FBI counterintelligence agents caught Gusev in the act when he made his final visit to the Washington, D.C., park bench in December 1999. Gusev didn't know it would be his final visit. He had no idea he was being closely watched. A few seconds after he sat down and put his hand into his coat pocket, agents with a radio-signal detector picked up a low-frequency transmission coming from the State Department, indicating that Gusev had activated a bug. When agents moved in on their target, they discovered the remote-control device in Gusev's pocket, and later a receiver and recorder in a Kleenex box on the dashboard of his car.

FBI agents questioned Gusev about his eavesdropping devices, but he wouldn't admit to anything illegal. Since Gusev was under protection of diplomatic immunity, he could not be arrested or punished. Gusev was released to the Russian Embassy staff three hours after being seized, and told to be out of the country within ten days.

Now it was up to the FBI to locate the bug concealed in the State Department building. There were thousands of places to hide a tiny listening device. A team of agents moved through the building floor by floor, room by room, inch by inch. The electronic devices the team used in their search are called brooms, since they can quickly sweep a room for bugs. The broom energizes any bugs in the room, which then give off a telltale signal that the broom immediately detects.

The FBI team moved up through the building, floor by floor. They had no luck until they swept a seventh floor high-security conference room and discovered a tiny microphone-transmitter powered by long-life batteries. The bug was concealed in a length of wall molding. Agents tested Gusev's triggering device and found that, as expected, it activated the bug. For months, Gusev had been using it to gather secret intelligence for the Russians. Agents removed the tiny device, and the State Department was debugged.

Besides sophisticated technology, the FBI also used clever detective work to apprehend Gusev. He was originally spotted by a special CIA surveillance unit known as the "G"s. Disguised as everything from window washers to homeless people, the Gs anonymously patrol the streets around Washington, D.C., government buildings looking for foreign intelligence officers. To become one of the Gs, you must have a good memory for faces. Gs are supplied with photographs of employees of foreign embassies and consulates who are suspected of being spies. The Gs first noticed Gusev when they remembered his face from a photograph. They put him under surveillance, following him on a regular basis because of his suspicious behavior. The Gs noticed that Gusev was a frequent visitor to the park near the State Department. On each visit he would pull into the same parking spot, sit on the same park bench with his hand in his pocket for a while, then return to his car, which had diplomatic plates, and drive back to the Russian Embassy.

While the Gs were shadowing Gusev, they were taking extra care to remain invisible to their target. Being a spy himself, Gusev would be on the lookout for surveillance. He would use well-known countersurveillance techniques to make sure that he wasn't being followed. But as careful as he was, Gusev wasn't careful enough.

COUNTERESPIONAGE IN ACTION

Sometimes even the most determined and clever use of countersurveillance techniques isn't enough, not if the agents following you are as clever as you are. This was the case with Harold James Nicholson, a CIA agent who photographed secret U.S. documents and sold them to Russian intelligence.

Nicholson was engaged in counterespionage, the penetration of an opponent's intelligence agency. In this case, the opponent was the United States. Nicholson was a CIA officer working *for* Russia, the nation he was supposed to be working *against*.

As an intelligence officer, Nicholson was well-versed in the tradecraft techniques of countersurveillance. On June 27, 1996, at 10:11 A.M., he left his Singapore hotel room carrying his camera bag, as if he were a tourist out to take pictures. For the next four hours Nicholson made his way around the city not to take pictures, but to make sure he was not being followed. A CIA document presented at Nicholson's trial stated that "Nicholson was observed taking numerous countersurveillance measures, such as backtracking his steps, watching glass panels of shops to look behind him, then entering and immediately exiting a subway station. During this excursion, Nicholson made no purchases and took no photographs."[2]

Nicholson went out again that same evening. CIA agents were again watching as a man met him at a subway station and took him to a car. The CIA trial document described the meeting: "The trunk of the car opened, and Nicholson placed his camera bag in the trunk. Nicholson then got into the back seat of the vehicle. The vehicle bore diplomatic license plates which are registered to the Russian Embassy in Singapore. The vehicle left the area. This meeting with Russian nationals was not authorized, nor did Nicholson report it to the CIA as required by agency regulations."[3]

Harold James Nicholson was arrested by the FBI in November 1996 and charged with committing espionage for Russia. FBI agents arrested him in a Washington, D.C., airport as he headed for a secret meeting in Europe with his Russian intelligence handlers. When FBI agents searched Nicholson, they found rolls of exposed film containing Top Secret information. In March 1997, Harold James Nicholson pleaded guilty to selling secrets to the Russian Federation Foreign Intelligence Service (SVRR) and was sentenced to 23 years in prison.

MOLES

Nicholson was a double agent, an agent working for the SVRR and against the CIA, which had originally hired him. His job was to pass secret information about CIA operations to the SVRR while making the CIA believe that he was still being loyal to them. Nicholson had the advantage of all double agents: He was being paid by both sides at once. But he was also under a double dose of pressure: to keep both sides convinced that he was being loyal to their agency and their agency only.

Nicholson was a special kind of double agent. He was a *mole*. A mole is a double agent who is also an intelligence officer. While supposedly working for one intelligence agency, the mole secretly works on behalf of an opponent agency.

ROBERT HANSSEN

On February 18, 2001, Robert Hanssen was arrested by FBI agents. Hanssen, 56 years old, was with the FBI himself. In fact, he was one of its highest-ranking agents. Hanssen had served as deputy director of the FBI Intelligence Division's Soviet section, a position that gave him access to a great many secrets. David Major, who worked with him for 20 years, said that Hanssen had access to "all sources, all methods, all techniques, all targets. There's only a few people in counterintelligence that have to know everything. And he was one of them."[4]

Hanssen was arrested in the process of delivering a garbage bag full of classified documents to Russian intelligence agents. Hanssen planned to exchange the documents for a bag containing $50,000 in cash waiting for him at a dead drop location in the park. Instead, he found FBI agents waiting for him.

FBI intelligence officer Hanssen had been selling U.S. secrets to Russian intelligence officers for 15 years before he was caught. After arresting Hanssen, the FBI launched an investigation to figure out how he could have been an FBI mole for so many years without being discovered. As unlikely as it seems, though, this was not the first time that a high-ranking U.S. intelligence officer had gotten way with selling secrets to the Russians for years. The same thing had happened in the case of CIA intelligence officer Aldrich Ames.

THE MAKING OF A MOLE

Aldrich Hazen Ames joined the CIA on a full-time basis in 1962 at the age of 21, but the story of his betrayal begins twenty-three years later in 1985. Until then, Ames was a loyal

CIA intelligence officer. He was not a good one, though. Ames had been reprimanded by his superiors on several occasions, and his job evaluations were consistently poor.

Yet Ames kept getting promoted to positions of higher and higher authority within the CIA. This should not have happened. If any of his superiors had taken a thorough look at Ames's record, Ames never would have been promoted. For one reason or another—no one has ever been able to explain exactly why—no one ever did. The CIA kept moving Ames up the ladder, giving him more and more responsibility, which gave him access to more and more classified information. By 1985, Ames had access to the names of every CIA intelligence officer and secret agent engaged in espionage operations against the Soviet Union. Ames now possessed one of the two primary characteristics of a mole: access to super-secret information of great value to the enemy.

The other characteristic is instability, and Aldrich Ames had plenty of that as well, both professionally and in his personal life. Ames was bitter about his job, deeply in debt, and battling marital and drinking problems.

DEFECTION

Ames knew how he might solve his financial and marital problems while getting revenge on the CIA and the United States of America, all at once. In April 1985 he walked into the Soviet Embassy in New York City and volunteered his services to the KGB, the Russian intelligence service, as a mole for the Soviet Union.

The Soviets were only too happy to accept Ames's offer. Ames was in charge of all CIA operations against Soviet intelligence outside the Soviet Union, and he knew the names of every single secret agent working against the Soviet Union.

Ames knew he was sealing many of these men's doom when he turned their names over to Soviet intelligence. During an interview with author David Wise, after Ames had been caught and put in prison, Ames admitted he knew these secret agents would be either executed or condemned to prison. But he felt he had no choice at the time. "It was my own sense of failure, inadequacy, and fear that made me conceive of it [his dilemma] as even greater than it was in reality."[5]

On June 13, 1985, in his fourth floor CIA office, Ames wrapped several pounds of Top Secret information in plastic bags, took the elevator to the ground floor, and walked out. Ames should not have been able to take this information from the CIA building. Guards should have stopped him and checked it. If they had, it would have been taken from Ames and he would have been placed under immediate arrest. But Ames knew that the CIA no longer examined packages carried from the building.

Ames then took the plastic bags holding the greatest amount of highly classified information ever given to the KGB in a single meeting and turned it over to his new Soviet handlers in a Washington, D.C., restaurant. In exchange, the KGB gave Aldrich Ames two million dollars. His financial problems were solved, but Ames now had a new set of problems. He had betrayed his country. After this, he said, he realized that "what I had done could never be undone and . . . I would be forever at hazard because of it."[6] Ames knew that the crime he had just committed could never be forgiven. There was no turning back.

CARELESSNESS ON BOTH SIDES

Aldrich Ames remained a mole for the next nine years, keeping his high-level CIA job and selling sensitive CIA secrets to the Soviets. Between fall 1985 and spring 1986, twenty CIA agents in the Soviet Union disappeared as a result of his actions. And more kept disappearing. The CIA went to work to solve this problem and kept working at it year after year without success.

Ames was under constant suspicion. He failed to pass lie detector tests in which he was asked about his loyalty to America. And CIA agents kept looking into his financial situation. Ames had claimed that his newfound wealth came from his wife's parents, who lived in Bogota, Colombia. An agent sent to investigate the family's financial state did a careless job, mistaking a rich uncle and aunt of Ames's wife for her parents.

Suspicions remained but were not acted upon. An intelligence officer who investigated the Ames affair after Ames was caught said that one reason Ames was able to get away with his spying for so long was denial on the part of the CIA. The CIA did not want to have to admit that the guilty party was one of their own, the investigator said, especially an officer who had attained such a high position of trust as Aldrich Ames. A revelation like that would have been embarrassing for the CIA. And the longer the mystery dragged on, the more embarrassing the revelation would have been.

CLOSING IN

Finally, by the spring of 1992, the evidence against Ames was too overwhelming to ignore or deny. A check of his bank and credit-card records showed an enormous flow of money in and out of his accounts over the years, and the big cash deposits matched up exactly with the dates on which Ames had taken trips to Russia. Between 1985 and 1993, Ames and his wife managed to spend $1.4 million and to accumulate credit card bills of $455,000. With this evidence, the CIA had to admit that one of their own was the mole who had been eluding them for nine long years.

CIA officers do not have the legal power to arrest anyone. The arrest of Aldrich Ames had to be carried out by FBI agents. But instead of arresting him immediately, the FBI and CIA put Ames and his family under months of intense surveillance. They hoped to catch him red-handed, actually handing over secret documents to the Soviets.

But Ames was extremely cautious when it came to his espionage activities. To get secret information into the hands of his Soviet handlers, he used dead drops near his home, in a suburb of Washington, D.C., that were remote and hard to keep under surveillance. Not even the Gs could catch Ames in the act.

Meanwhile, the FBI was busy gathering evidence from other angles. In August 1993, after being granted court approval, they set up wiretaps on Ames's house, monitoring his calls. They secretly installed an electronic transmitter known as a "beacon" on Ames's Jaguar so they could track it. In September, they began keeping a 24-hour eye on Ames's front door with a concealed video camera known as "the Eye." Around the same time, they began using Trashint, secretly searching Ames's garbage. In October, while Ames and his wife were away, agents broke into Ames's house and installed bugs, again after obtaining a court order based on evidence that Ames was engaged in counterespionage.

They also had obtained a court order to search the house, and the search yielded more evidence, some from papers in desk drawers and some from Ames's computer hard drive. The agents were careful to put everything back where it belonged. They were gone in a matter of hours.

The FBI searched Ames's office at the CIA Building as well, after obtaining permission from the U.S. Attorney General. At this time Ames was assigned to the Directorate of Intelligence Counternarcotics Center. Any secret documents in his office should have related directly to his work of countering the flow of narcotics into the United States, but a number of documents did not relate to this work, including secret information on nuclear submarines.

THE CAPTURE

February 21, 1994, was Presidents' Day, a federal holiday, and CIA offices were officially closed. The next day Ames was scheduled to make a CIA–sponsored trip to Russia as part of his work. No one knew whether Ames suspected that he was

Aldrich Ames, under arrest, in 1994.

under suspicion, but if he did, he might stay in Russia and never return. Ames was at home packing for the trip when he received a phone call from his CIA boss, David Edger. "We have some hot information. You better get in here," Edger said.[7]

Ames was driving toward CIA headquarters when FBI cars surrounded his Jaguar and pulled him over. The arrest took just 45 seconds. Ames was handcuffed and taken directly to an FBI office that had been specially prepared with pictures of the dead drops he'd used to pass information to his Soviet handlers tacked to the walls. John F. Lewis, Jr., a veteran FBI counter-intelligence agent, was there when Ames arrived. "When they brought him in, he looked like the wind was knocked out of him. He was asked to sit down. When he looked around at the walls, his head sank. And he wouldn't look up."[8]

If the United States had been at war, Ames might have been sentenced to death. Ames was fortunate that there is no death penalty for espionage in peacetime. On April 28, 1994, Aldrich Hazen Ames pleaded guilty and was sentenced to life in prison without possibility of parole.

Some of Ames's victims were not so fortunate. Ames betrayed a total of 36 CIA and other allied secret agents, which resulted in at least ten of them being executed. One of Ames's victims, Valery Martynov, was put to death by a Soviet firing squad on May 28, 1987, at the age of 41.

As Ames himself said, espionage "almost always involves a betrayal of trust."[9] Espionage rests on shaky moral and ethical ground, and this can make for a great deal of controversy.

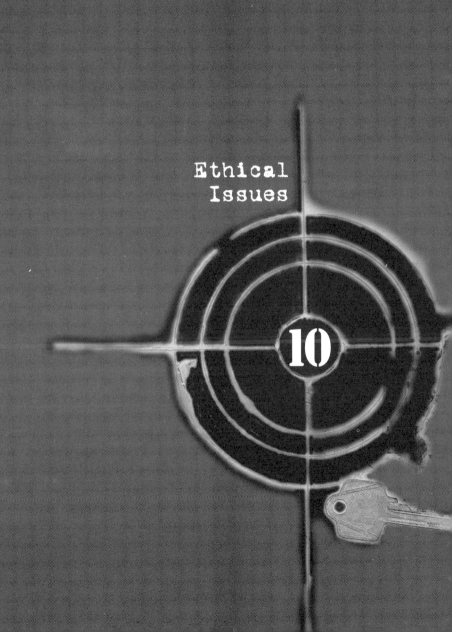

Ethical
Issues

10

Antonio J. Mendez sits in a chair in an office at CIA headquarters in Langley, Virginia. Mendez is interviewing for a job with the CIA. "How would you feel about telling a lie for the good of your country?" his interviewer asks. Mendez thinks a moment and then answers, "A lie can be a deceitful way to hurt people. Or it can be a necessary form of deception in time of war. I think we're engaged in war, and both sides are using deception."[1]

Mendez's interview took place in April 1965, in the midst of the Cold War. While the United States and the Soviet Union were not engaged in actual physical conflict, they were fighting a psychological war. And if telling lies meant helping to win that war, then to Mendez's way of thinking, lying was justified.

Now that the Cold War is over and the Soviets have been defeated, are secret agents still justified in telling lies as part of their espionage operations? Most members of the intelligence community would say yes, since we are still at war with other enemies, such as terrorists, narcotics traffickers, and foreign spies engaged in industrial espionage against the United States.

But to what extent can lying and other forms of deception be permitted in espionage work? When are lies told by secret agents truly necessary, and when are they deceitful and hurtful? What are the limits on espionage in peacetime America?

ESPIONAGE IN A CLOSED SOCIETY

In a closed society, such as North Korea, Sri Lanka, or Myanmar, the government exerts more control over the lives of its citizens than in an open society, such as the United States. In closed societies, citizens are not guaranteed protection against their government. Tactics such as press censorship, wiretaps, surveillance, and strong-armed interrogation of citizens are a part of daily life. Newspapers, television, and radio may publish only stories that the government approves of, and the government may impose restrictions and bans on public rallies and meetings.

This was the case in the nation of Myanmar, where government authorities put the chief opposition leader, Aung San Suu Kyi, under house arrest in 1988. Despite this, she led her National League for Democracy party to an overwhelming victory in the 1990 national elections. But Myanmar's ruling military regime refused to step down. As of May 2001, Aung San Suu Kyi was still being held.

In a closed society like this, secret agencies are vital to the ruling government, which uses them to keep a close eye on its citizens, especially anyone who dares to oppose the ruling government. In a closed society, espionage is a tool that the government uses to protect itself against its citizens and keep itself in power.

ESPIONAGE IN AN OPEN SOCIETY

In general, citizens in an open society regard the use of secret agencies to spy on citizens as a dangerous misuse of power. The Bill of Rights of the U.S. Constitution guarantees all citizens protection from government interference in their private lives. This makes for an uncomfortable relationship between U.S. secret agencies and U.S. citizens, including many government officials. Henry Stimson, President Herbert Hoover's Secretary of State, went so far as to shut down the State Department's code-breaking office in 1929. The reason he gave was that "Gentlemen do not read each other's mail."[2]

Secret agencies have remained objects of mistrust in America, a mistrust that runs so deep that it gives birth to wild rumors. One of these rumors insists that instead of fighting the flow of narcotics into the United Ststes, the CIA actually helps bring narcotics in and profits from their sales. Another anti–CIA rumor says that in 1947 outer-space aliens landed near Roswell, New Mexico, and that the CIA immediately took them captive and has been holding them prisoner ever since. As unlikely as these rumors sound, they persist because of Americans' perpetual distrust of secret agencies and espionage.

On the other hand, defenders of the CIA and other secret agencies argue that secrecy does have a legitimate place in an open society. That place is not to help keep the ruling government in power, as in Myanmar, but to help protect national security. And national security must be protected in peacetime, as well as in times of war. There are terrorists and narcotics traffickers to deal with and foreign intelligence services engaging in industrial espionage within the United States.

CROSSING THE LINE

The case of Aldrich Ames shows that there are occasions when U.S. secret agencies are justified in spying on their own citizens. Ames's espionage work on behalf of Russia was a threat to national security. As serious as the Ames case was, CIA and

FBI agents were careful to obtain the required court orders for the eavesdropping and searches they conducted on Ames's home and office. They could not spy on Ames, an American citizen, simply because he disagreed in some way with the U.S. government. By law CIA and FBI agents were required to show the court that Ames presented a legitimate threat to national security.

The CIA and FBI have not always been so careful. For a time, in fact, they behaved recklessly in regard to spying on American citizens. This was during the Vietnam War years, in the late 1960s and early 1970s, when thousands of Americans were protesting the presence of American troops in Vietnam. Thousands of antiwar protesters became subjects of CIA and FBI spying, including high-profile celebrities such as movie star Jane Fonda and poet Allen Ginsberg.

Lyndon Johnson and Richard Nixon were Presidents during these years. Top officials in their administrations believed that many of these antiwar protesters were controlled by the enemy, the North Vietnamese and the Soviets. They saw antiwar protesters as genuine threats to national security.

During these years the CIA compiled files on over 13,000 individuals as part of a secret action known as Operation CHAOS. CIA agents monitored all antiwar demonstrations in the Washington, D.C., area and infiltrated antiwar organizations. CIA actions against antiwar protesters included surveillance, burglaries, criminal frame-ups, and disinformation campaigns. But when all was said and done, Operation CHAOS unearthed no evidence indicating that any antiwar protesters were controlled by any foreign enemy.

CONGRESSIONAL OVERSIGHT

The CIA has always been forbidden by Congress from engaging in domestic spying. The illegal CIA activities of Operation CHAOS were first revealed to the public in 1974 in a series of newspaper articles by *The New York Times* reporter Seymour Hersh. The articles sparked congressional hearings on CIA activities the next year, led by Senator Frank Church of Idaho. Once the Church Committee evidence was in, government investigators accused the CIA of conducting espionage against the people they were pledged to protect, American citizens.

Perhaps if the CIA had uncovered any real evidence of enemy control of antiwar protesters, the agency would not have been judged so harshly. But there was no such evidence. The CIA had no excuses for its illegal activities. Before the Church Committee hearings, the CIA had conducted its operations in near total secrecy—like a nation unto itself, some critics said. After the 1975 hearing, things changed for the CIA and the rest of the U.S. intelligence community as well. These changes were summed up by Congress under the term *oversight*.

Ironically, "oversight" has two distinct and opposite meanings. The first is "failure to notice or think of something," which comes close to describing the treatment the CIA received from Congress before 1975—failing to notice or think of it. The other meaning of oversight, the one Congress intended, is "watchful care." From 1975 on, the CIA would receive watchful care from Congress.

By July 1977, two congressional oversight committees were in place, the Senate Select Committee on Intelligence (SCIC) and the House Permanent Select Committee on Intelligence (HPSCI). The task of these committees was to investigate allegations of illegal or improper activities. Members of Congress appointed to these committees had full and complete access to all classified materials of the CIA, as well as the other twelve intelligence agencies. The CIA was no longer a nation unto itself.

ECHELON CONCERNS

Even when secret agencies stay within their proper boundaries, they still operate outside the boundaries other citizens must operate within. They still engage in espionage operations that raise controversy.

One of these controversial operations is the National Security Agency's Project Echelon (see Chapter 4, "Intercepting Comint"). This worldwide Techint surveillance operation, which can intercept virtually all the world's communications, has become a cause for concern worldwide. The French, for instance, said that they strongly suspect the United States is using Echelon to engage in industrial espionage against their nation. U.S. State Department spokesman James Rubin replied that "U.S. intelligence agencies are not tasked to engage in industrial espionage, or obtain trade secrets for the benefit of any U.S. company or companies."[3]

Echelon has also made American citizens uneasy. Some fear Echelon will be used to spy on them. House Republican Bob Barr said, "I am concerned that there are not sufficient legal mechanisms in place to protect our private information from unauthorized eavesdropping through such mechanisms as Project Echelon."[4]

The NSA replied to these concerns with a February 2000 letter to members of Congress: "We want to assure you that the NSA's activities are conducted in accordance with the highest constitutional, legal and ethical standards, and in compliance with statutes and regulations designed to protect the privacy rights of U.S. persons."[5]

CARNIVORE CONCERNS

The FBI also operates a Techint program that, like Echelon, has become a cause for concern. Carnivore is the FBI's Internet surveillance system, a high-tech software program that allows law enforcement agents to intercept and analyze vast amounts of e-mail.

E-mail is sent through an Internet service provider (ISP), a kind of Internet post office. When Carnivore software is placed at an ISP, it scans all incoming and outgoing e-mails. Unlike Echelon, Carnivore does not look at the messages themselves. It does not scan messages for key words or phrases. Instead, Carnivore examines only the e-mail address, looking for addresses of people who have been targeted as part of a criminal investigation. When an e-mail to or from a targeted address shows up, Carnivore captures it as intelligence, while ignoring all other messages.

Modern criminals of many varieties rely heavily on e-mail in their illegal operations. Carnivore gathers intelligence for investigations involving counterterrorism, counternarcotics, Internet fraud, computer hacking, global organized crime, and more.

Objections to Carnivore show Americans' persistent distrust of secret agencies. Barry Steinhardt, associate director of the American Civil Liberties Union, a nonprofit organization that looks out for people's civil rights and freedoms, said that citizens shouldn't trust that Carnivore will be used only against criminal suspects. FBI spokesman Steven Berry replied that Carnivore gives the FBI "a surgical ability to intercept and collect the communications which are the subject of a court order," and that Carnivore ignores everything else.[6]

COVERT OPERATIONS

Secret agencies are in the business of gathering and analyzing information. They are not in the business of taking direct action. There is one exception to this rule, though. This exception is known as *covert operations*.

Espionage is at the heart of covert operations. These operations are like espionage because they are both secret and illegal. But intelligence officers and secret agents engaged in covert operations take espionage a step further. Instead of gathering information in secret, they take action in secret.

They usually take these secret actions against a foreign leader or military force. Covert actions range from circulating propaganda leaflets to influence the outcome of another nation's elections, to training and fighting alongside a rebel army.

All covert operations are designed and executed with two goals in mind. First, the public is never supposed to find out about the operation. But if word does leak out, then U.S. heads of government will be able to plausibly—believably—deny that they had anything to do with the operation.

The CIA is in charge of planning and carrying out covert operations. They fall somewhere between diplomacy and full-scale military action. Only the President may direct the CIA to undertake a covert operation, and only when national security is at stake.

COVERT FAILURES

Covert operations are intended to be used strictly as a last resort and only if they have a good chance of both succeeding and remaining secret. A surprising number of covert operations have failed to meet these criteria, some in spectacular fashion.

The most notorious of failed covert operations was the Bay of Pigs invasion. In 1961 the CIA financed and directed an invasion of Fidel Castro's Cuba by 1,500 Cuban exiles. President John F. Kennedy authorized the invasion with the goal of overthrowing Castro, Cuba's Communist dictator. By using Cuban exiles, people who had emigrated to the United States from Cuba, instead of U.S. troops, Kennedy could plausibly deny that the United States had anything to do with the invasion.

The invasion was a failure. Castro's forces easily defeated the CIA–directed exiles. The cover was blown and the whole world knew of the CIA's involvement. Later, in an official report on the failed operation, the CIA blamed itself, citing its own arrogance, ignorance, and incompetence, and promised that from then on the job of overthrowing enemies would belong not to the CIA but to U.S. military forces.

The CIA violated this promise in the 1980s in another failed covert operation known as Iran-Contra. The administration of President Ronald Reagan directed the CIA to secretly sell weapons to Iran in exchange for hostages Iran was holding. The monies would be used to provide weapons and

Lt. Col. Oliver North holds up a National Security Council Intelligence document marked Top Secret during the Iran-Contra hearings. North used the Top Secret designation to defend his keeping information from Congress.

training for the Contras, rebel forces opposing the ruling government of Nicaragua. Both these actions were expressly forbidden by Congress, so the Reagan administration tried to do them secretly through CIA covert operations. Money skimmed from the illegal arms sales to Iran was used to illegally aid the Contras. The cover on both these illegal operations was blown, giving the American public a fresh new set of reasons to distrust secret agencies.

WHEN ARE COVERT OPERATIONS JUSTIFIED?

Iran-Contra happened after the congressional oversight committees were established. By law, any plans for covert operations had to be submitted to the oversight committees for approval. The Reagan administration violated this law when they bypassed the committees and went directly to the CIA. While the public blamed the Reagan administration for Iran-Contra, they also blamed the CIA.

Exactly when to use covert operations remains an extremely controversial issue. At one extreme are those who believe that covert operations are totally unethical and should never be used in any situation. At the opposite extreme are those who believe that virtually any use of secret agencies in defense of national security is ethically acceptable, including covert operations. As long as the end result is keeping U.S. citizens safe from foreign threats, the consequences are not important. This attitude is often phrased as "The end justifies the means." G. Gordon Liddy, a former CIA officer who took part in covert operations, believes that they are justified because, unethical or not, other nations do the same things. "The world isn't Beverly Hills," he says. "It's a bad neighborhood at two o'clock in the morning."[7]

In between these two extremes are compromise positions on instances when covert operations are justified. These instances generally involve humanitarian aid, such as helping people who face enslavement, torture, or genocide. Many, if not most, government officials would at least consider the use of covert operations in these cases. But aside from humanitarian instances, there seems to be little agreement on when or whether to use covert operations.

SEEKING NEW POWERS

G. Gordon Liddy's statement about the world being a "bad neighborhood" was echoed by Vice President Dick Cheney. "It is a mean, nasty, dangerous, dirty business out there," he said. Cheney spoke shortly after the September 11, 2001, terrorist airline hijackings in New York City and Washington, D.C., that left thousands dead.

Cheney was reacting to limits on whom the CIA could recruit as secret agents. CIA field officers were not allowed to recruit people involved in actual terrorism. "If you're only going to work with officially approved, certified good guys, you are not going to find out what the bad guys are doing," he said.[8]

Cheney, Secretary of State Colin Powell, and other members of the Bush administration were seeking new powers to aid the intelligence community in fighting the war on terrorism. These new powers included loosening restrictions on FBI surveillance set by congressional oversight committees in the 1970s.

The United States had just declared a war on terrorists all around the world. Yet the Bush administration's calls for new powers in the name of national security were met by opposition from organizations dedicated to guarding civil liberties, such as the American Civil Liberties Union. The uneasy relationship between U.S. secret agencies and U.S. citizens seems destined to continue no matter what happens in the future.

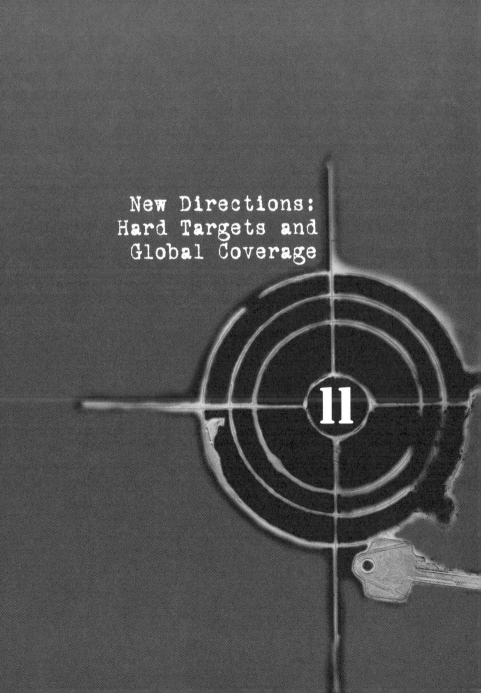

New Directions:
Hard Targets and
Global Coverage

11

Intelligence experts agree that since the Cold War ended, intelligence gathering and espionage have changed in a number of ways, especially when it comes to targets. During the Cold War years, between 1945 and 1991, espionage was simple in this respect: You knew what your primary target was. If you were a member of a U.S. secret agency, that target was the Soviet Union. If you were a member of a Soviet secret agency, it was the United States. There were no other primary targets. The two superpowers, which together dominated world politics, continually battled each other to see who would prevail, and espionage was an important part of the battle plans on both sides.

With the 1991 breakup of the Soviet Union into 14 separate countries, the United States prevailed. Former CIA Director James Woolsey referred to the defeated Soviet Union as the great Soviet dragon, which the U.S. had slain. Woolsey referred to all the new targets facing U.S. secret agencies as "a bewildering variety of poisonous snakes that have been let loose in a dark jungle."[1]

President Bill Clinton's CIA director, George Tenet, said that the immediate goal of the U.S. intelligence community "is to make sense of a world that is more complicated and less predictable than it ever has been in our history."[2] To help make sense of this new set of post-Cold War intelligence and espionage targets, President Clinton signed Presidential Decision Directive 35 (PDD-35). This 1995 document divides secret agency coverage into two main categories: hard targets and global coverage.

Hard targets include rogue nations, terrorists, and global organized crime. Global coverage includes information warfare, environmental degradation, and peacekeeping.

HARD TARGET: ROGUE NATIONS

Rogue nations defy the rule of law and international agreements. They are known for their aggressive and unpredictable behavior toward neighboring nations and toward the United States (see Chapter 6, "A Controversial Report").

The top priority of U.S. secret agencies toward rogue nations is to monitor their production of weapons of mass destruction (WMD). Conventional weapons, that is bullets or bombs, do most of their damage in a few seconds. Weapons of mass destruction keep on killing. They can make entire regions of the world uninhabitable for years on end. These weapons fall into three classes: chemical, biological, and nuclear. Chemical WMD, such as nerve gases, are manufactured in laboratories. Biological WMD, such the infectious disease anthrax, are made from bacteria found in nature. The thought of weapons of mass destruction in the hands of aggressive, unpredictable nations is cause for alarm.

The most widespread and potentially deadly class of WMD is nuclear arms. As of 2001, some two dozen nations were actively engaged in the production or attainment of nuclear arms. Cuba, Iran, Iraq, Libya, and North Korea were among the rogue nations with the capability of producing nuclear WMD.[3]

One of the duties of secret agencies is to gather intelligence to help stop nations from producing nuclear weapons. A special Nonproliferation Intelligence Center has been set up to address the problem of the spread of nuclear weapons.

Intelligence officers and secret agents assigned to nonproliferation duties work on keeping track of existing nuclear materials, such as weapons-grade plutonium, that could be used to produce nuclear arms. Russia has a huge supply of nuclear materials left over from the Cold War years. If these materials were to reach rogue nations, the results might not be in the best interests of the United States. Secret agencies also monitor nations that already have the capability of producing nuclear weapons, so these agencies can warn U.S. government officials of any attempts to test these weapons, and any preparations to possibly use nuclear weapons against the United States (see Chapter 3, "Spies in the Sky").

Attending to these nonproliferation duties requires a network of carefully coordinated spy satellites along with photogrammetrists and image interpreters to make sense of satellite imagery. It also requires spies who are knowledgeable in science as well as in traditional secret agent tradecraft, and economists who can trace the worldwide flow of money used to buy weapons materials.

At present, no rogue states appear to have the kinds of aircraft needed to deliver a nuclear bomb or, with the possible exception of North Korea, the long-range missiles needed to carry a nuclear warhead to its target.

But secret agencies remain on the lookout for a more low-tech nuclear device known as a "suitcase bomb." The U.S. actually had such a weapon in its nuclear arsenal until 1989. It was known as the "Special Atomic Demolition Munition." It weighed about 60 pounds (27 kilograms) and could be carried in a backpack.[4] This is the kind of nuclear weapon that could possibly be delivered by a terrorist.

HARD TARGET: TERRORISTS

Terrorism is the criminal use or threat of violence to create public fear and anxiety. Terrorists kidnap and kill innocent victims. They believe their violence is justified because their actions are in the name of a cause, which is often ethnic or religious hatred.

Intelligence officers and secret agents attempt to identify terrorist groups, locate the primary bases from which they operate, and warn government leaders of any planned terrorist attacks. A special Counterterrorism Center has been set up to coordinate their efforts.

FBI counterterrorism experts gather intelligence about terrorist attacks involving Americans and track down the terrorists responsible for the attacks. In February 1993, an explosion rocked the World Trade Center in New York City. Six people were killed and more than a thousand were wounded. The explosion came from a bomb planted in a van in the World Trade Center parking garage.

FBI counterterrorism experts immediately suspected a terrorist bombing. They combed the wreckage and found an axle from the van that had held the bomb. The axle had the van's vehicle identification number (VIN) stamped on it. FBI experts used the VIN to trace the van to a rental agency in New York City. From there, they tracked down the man who had rented the van. He was one of the terrorist bombers.

Four years later, following a worldwide manhunt, FBI counterterrorism experts tracked down the five other terrorists responsible for the bombing and brought them to justice. The six terrorists, all of Middle Eastern origin, had planted the bomb to seek revenge for America's continuing support of their enemy, the nation of Israel.

On October 12, 2000, two terrorists attacked a U.S. Navy warship. The *USS Cole* was in the process of refueling in the port of Aden, the capital city of Yemen, in southwest Arabia.

At 11:18 A.M., the two suicide bombers drove their motorized skiff into the warship, tearing a 40-by-40-foot (1,220-by-1,220-centimeter) hole in its side. Investigators concluded that a powerful plastic explosive had been used. Potential suspects included members of several Middle Eastern terrorist groups. Seventeen U.S. sailors were killed and 39 more wounded in the attack. According to the U.S. State Department, this was one of 423 terrorist attacks worldwide in 2000, compared with 392 in 1999.

Terrorists are taking advantage of advances in communication technology. Speaking of modern terrorists, CIA official John Gannon said, "Chances are they will be using laptop computers, establishing their own Web sites, and using sophisticated encryption, reconnaissance, and weaponry their predecessors could not have imagined."[5]

Gannon's remarks also apply to the network of terrorists who planned the September 11, 2001, attacks that left thousands dead. Early intelligence reports indicated that the hijackers, operating in several different cities, kept in contact by computer e-mail.

HARD TARGET: GLOBAL ORGANIZED CRIME

Since the breakup of the Soviet Union in 1991, organized crime has turned more and more global in nature. Two chief reasons are the advance of technology, especially communications technology, and the explosive growth of narcotics consumption in the United States.

Secret agencies, with the help of both spies and satellite imagery, can locate drug-processing factories in South America and Mexico. They can identify jungle landing strips, drug laboratories, and storage areas. Using information gathered by U.S. spy satellite imagery, Colombian soldiers seized 22 tons of cocaine in a single raid in 1994. But these drug laboratories are small and mobile, and there are many of them.

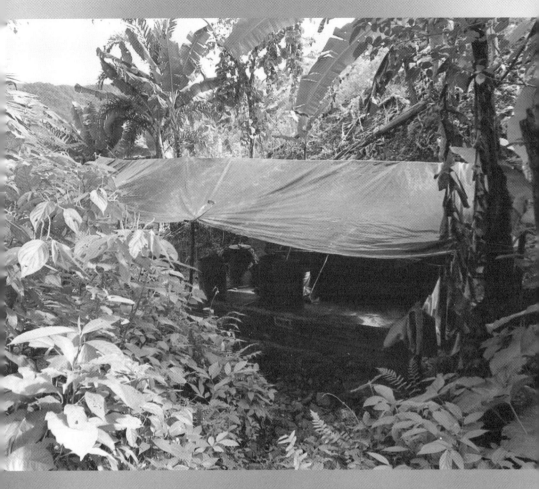

This cocaine lab in Colombia is virtually invisible by air, and you'd need an expert tracker to find it in the jungle.

Besides concentrating on the production and transportation of narcotics, secret agencies work on monitoring the flow of narco-dollars. Every day, drug lords and their organizations, known as cartels, transfer their profits electronically to dozens of banks around the world. Drug lords can use computers to transfer their vast sums of money to secure banks thousands of miles away in a matter of minutes.

Intelligence analyst Patrick Hughes writes, "The international drug trade is becoming more complex as new areas of drug cultivation and transit continue to emerge and international criminal syndicates take advantage of rapid advancements in global communications, transportation, and finance to mask their illicit operations."[6]

GLOBAL COVERAGE: INFORMATION WARFARE

While the hard targets of rogue states, terrorists, and global organized crime were not prominent targets during the Cold War years, they were still among the concerns of secret agencies. Their prominence is new, but not their presence.

Today a newer set of targets has emerged since the Cold War years. President Clinton has classified these new targets under the blanket term "global coverage." One of these new targets is information warfare. Billions of dollars are spent every year to strengthen U.S. computer networks and to exploit the computer networks of U.S. opponents. How important are these networks to daily life in the United States? A system of interlocking computer networks regulates communications, commerce, and defense. If these networks were to be successfully invaded and tampered with, the nation's banking system, air-traffic-control system, telecommunications network, and electric power grid, among other vital aspects of daily life, could be at serious risk.

How serious could things get? In 1993, computer hackers managed to break into the U.S. National Weather Service (NWS) computers and came close to shutting them down. If the hackers had succeeded, airlines would soon have been forced to shut down, since they depend on minute-by-minute weather updates and forecasts. John Ward, computer systems manager for the NWS, said that if the hackers had succeeded, "We would be talking in terms of tens of millions of dollars [of damage] per hour."[7]

The hackers failed, but FBI experts in computer counter-intelligence were waiting in case they should try again, and they did. When the next attacks on the NWS computers came, agents traced them across the Atlantic to Denmark, where seven young men were tracked down and arrested. The young men ranged in age from 17 to 24 and went by cybernicknames such as Wedlock, Zephyr, and Dixie. And they were not computer geniuses at all. The seven hackers had not invented any of the tactics they used to invade the NWS computers. They had downloaded all the information they needed from computer bulletin boards on the Internet.

The National Security Agency is the main intelligence agency responsible for information warfare. In 1995, the director of the NSA, Vice Admiral John M. McConnell, said, "We're more vulnerable [to computer espionage] than any other nation on Earth."[8] McConnell was referring to the fact that the United States is the most technologically advanced nation on Earth. Its national security is closely tied to a system of interlocking computer networks that are vulnerable to attack.

Six years later, McConnell's warning sounded like an eerie prediction. In May 2001, officials at the Pentagon revealed that the United States was undergoing a prolonged and serious cyber-attack from an unknown group of computer hackers. The offensive, which started in 1998, was codenamed Moonlight Maze by the Pentagon. Hackers involved in the offensive had used a cyber-warfare technique known as "tunneling" to steal sensitive data from computer systems at the U.S. military, the National Aeronautics and Space Administration, and several research laboratories and universities.

Russia is suspected of launching the attacks, but U.S. officials admitted they had very few clues to the identities of the Moonlight Maze hackers.

GLOBAL COVERAGE: ENVIRONMENTAL DEGRADATION

Environmental degradation is the second of the global coverage targets. In a way it is the most far-reaching, since it involves not just people, but the Earth itself. Environmental degradation is the ongoing damage to air, water, earth, and living things on the planet that occurs because of the influence of human activities. Unrestrained cutting down of trees to make farmland leads to erosion. Increased burning of fossil fuels, such as oil and gas, releases more and more carbon dioxide, which pollutes the air. More and more city slums built without sewage disposal systems lead to pollution of ground water.

As a result, more and more people around the world with little or no source of income find themselves living in flooded or drought-ridden or disease-ridden places. Environmental degradation is a serious threat to world stability, and therefore to the national security of every nation, including the United States.

U.S. intelligence agencies are gathering intelligence to identify nations that are doing harm to the environment, such as Russia dumping radioactive materials into the Arctic Ocean. By identifying these environmental threats, agencies can provide information that government leaders can use to put pressure on offending nations to change their environmental policies.

Much of the work in this area is done by the collecting of open-source intelligence and imagery from spy satellites. The long-range goal is to provide an ongoing supply of intelligence on the changing state of the planet, which leaders worldwide can use to counteract the effects of environmental degradation.

GLOBAL COVERAGE: PEACEKEEPING

This last target of global coverage involves the task of monitoring conflicts and peacekeeping agreements around the world. During the Cold War years, U.S. intelligence agencies had few resources to devote to conflicts in nations other than the Soviet Union or the nations it supported, such as Cuba and North Vietnam. The post–Cold War world is a different matter. Political scientist John Hedly said, "There are no obscure countries and remote regions anymore. The United States can suddenly be involved in a peacekeeping or humanitarian operation in Liberia or Somalia or Rwanda or Bosnia or Haiti."[9]

This new global approach to intelligence includes keeping track of the many ethnic, religious, and tribal conflicts occurring at any one moment around the world. And U.S. secret agencies use all the Humint and Techint techniques available to them to do this, including espionage.

CONCLUSION

Former Director of Central Intelligence William Colby said that good intelligence can replace "ignorance, fear and suspicion [with] knowledge and confidence." This was especially true during the Cold War years, when intelligence and espionage contributed to world peace, including the prevention of a catastrophic war between the United States and the Soviet Union.

Ironically, by stealing each other's secrets, the two opposing superpowers were able to get acquainted. Through espionage, each side came to know the capacities and intentions of the other, and that left less chance for misunderstanding that could lead to panic and war. By stealing each other's secrets, the United States and the Soviet Union came to know one another well enough to know just how far they could go. In this way, U.S. secret agencies had a stabilizing effect on world affairs during the tense Cold War years.

In their new post–Cold War, peacetime role, secret agencies may continue to have a similar effect. By tracing the effects of environmental degradation, including the spread of deadly diseases, and by providing intelligence on conflicts throughout the world, secret agencies have the potential to contribute to world peace.

Meanwhile, at home, U.S. citizens will continue to look at secret agencies in general and their use of espionage and covert operations in particular, with a suspicious eye. The uneasy relationship between secret agencies and the citizens of an open society will also continue.

Chapter Notes

Chapter One

1. Sun Tzu. *The Art of Warfare*. Translated by Lionel Giles. www.chinapage.com/sunzi-e.html.
2. Brown, Justin. "The Cold War Is Over, the Spy Game Isn't." *Christian Science Monitor*. December 10, 1999. www.fas.org/irp/news/1999/12/991210-bug.htm.
3. "About the National Security Agency." www.nsa.gov/about_nsa/index.html.
4. Wise, David. *Nightmover*. New York: HarperCollins Publishers, 1995, p. 225.

Chapter Two

1. Hulnick, Arthur S. *Fixing the Spy Machine: Preparing American Intelligence for the Twenty-First Century*. Westport, CT: Praeger Publishers, 1999, p. 174.
2. "Global Spy News." www.globalspy.com/SpyNews.htm.
3. Haynes, John Earl, and Harvey Klehr. *Venona: Decoding Soviet Espionage in America*. New Haven, CT: Yale University Press, 1999, pp. 288–289.
4. Fialka, John J. *War by Other Means: Economic Espionage in America*. New York: W.W. Norton & Company, 1997, p. 28.

Chapter Three

1. Broad, William J. "Spy Photos of Korea Missile Site Bring Dispute." *The New York Times*. January 11, 2000. www.nytimes.com/library/world/asia/011100nkorea-missle.html.
2. "USAF Fact Sheet." www.af.mil/news/factsheets/U_2S.html.
3. "Robots in the News." www.robotbooks.com/spy-fly-robot.html.

Chapter Four

1. "Interception Capabilities 2000." Directorate General for Research of the European Parliament. April, 1999. www.iptvreports.mcmail.com/ic2kreport.html.
2. Davis, Jack. "A Compendium of Analytic Tradecraft Notes." Central Intelligence Agency. intellit.muskingum.edu/intellsite/analysis_folder/di_catn_folder/foreword.html.
3. "Interception Capabilities 2000," ibid.
4. Johnson, Loch K., *Secret Agencies*. New Haven, CT: Yale University Press, 1996, p. 21.
5. "Interception Capabilities 2000," ibid.
6. Johnson, ibid, p. 20.

Chapter Five

1. Loeb, Vernon. "Foreseeing the Fall." *Washington Post*. November 19, 1999, p. A43.
2. Loeb, ibid, p. A43.
3. "Zimmermann Telegram." www.loyola.edu/dept/politics/icons/zimmer-d.jpg.
4. Freeh, Louis. "Encryption." Senate Judiciary Committee Hearing on Encryption. July 9, 1997. www.fbi.gov/congress/congress97/encrypt2.html.
5. Loeb, Vernon. "Back Channels." *Washington Post*. May 17, 2000, p. A25.
6. Davis, ibid.
7. "Soviet Active Measures in the 'Post-Cold War' Era: 1988–1991." United States Information Agency. June 1992. intellit.muskingum.edu/intellsite/russia_folder/pcw_era/sect_05.html.

Chapter Six

1. "Analytic Thinking and Presentation for Intelligence Producers." Central Intelligence Agency Office of Training and Education. 216.167.120.50/cia-ath/handbook01-07.zip.
2. "Analytic Thinking and Presentation for Intelligence Producers," ibid.

3. "Clinton to Leave NMD Decision to Successor." Channel News. July 27, 2000. 168.160.224.42/cover/storydb/2000/07/27/mn-nmd.727.html.

4. Diamond, Howard. "U.S. Intelligence Estimate Warns of Rising Missile Threats." *Arms Control Today*. September/October, 1999. www.armscontrol.org/ACT/sepoct99/nieso99.html.

5. Sciolino, Elaine, and Steven Lee Myers. "U.S. Study Reopens Division Over Nuclear Missile Threat." *The New York Times*. July 5, 2000. www.nytimes.com/library/world/global/070500missile-defense.html.

6. Park, Robert L. "Flash!! Clinton will not deploy a national missile defense." What's New. September 1, 2000. www.aps.org/WN/.

7. Gordon, Michael R. "Military Analysis: Grand Plan, Few Details." *The New York Times*. May 2, 2001. www.nytimes.com/21001/05/02/world/02MILI.html.

Chapter Seven

1. "The Intellgence Community." Central Intelligence Agency. www.odci.gov/ic/nro.html.

2. "State Department Report on Accidental Bombing of Chinese Embassy." July 6, 1999. www.usconsulate.org.hk/uscn/state/1999/0706.html.

3. "State Department Report on Accidental Bombing of Chinese Embassy," ibid.

4. "Combating Proliferation of Weapons of Mass Destruction." Report of the Commission to Assess the Organization of the Federal Government to Combat the Proliferation of Weapons of Mass Destruction. 1999. www.loyola.edu/dept/politics/intel/cpwmd1999.pdf.

5. "State Department Report on Accidental Bombing of Chinese Embassy," ibid.

6. Weiner, Tim, and James Risen. "Policy Makers, Diplomats, Intelligence Officers All Missed India's Intentions." *The New York Times*. May 25, 1998. www.mtholyoke.edu/acad/intrel/misintel.htm.

Chapter Eight

1. Freeh, Louis. "Hearing on Economic Espionage." House Judiciary Committee Subcommittee on Crime. May 9, 1996. www.fbi.gov/pressrm/congress/congress96/ecespio2.html.

2. Winkler, Ira. "The New Cold War Industrial Espionage." *Security Magazine*. April, 1998. www.scmagazine.com/scmagazine/1998_04/cover/cover.html.

3. Sevunts, Levon. "A Spy in the Office." *Montreal Gazette*. July 23, 2000. www.montrealgazette.com:80/news/pages/000723/4497311.homl.
4. Cohen, William. "Countering Industrial Espionage in the Post-Cold-War Era." United States Senate. June 24, 1992.
5. "Economic Espionage Act of 1996." United States House of Representatives. September 16, 1996. www.fas.org/irp/congress/1996_rpt/h104788.html.
6. Winkler, ibid.
7. Nelson, Jack. "U.S. Firms' '97 Losses to Spies Put at $300 Billion." *Los Angeles Times*. January 12, 1998. www.reactnetwork.com/econspy0111.html.
8. Kahaner, Larry. *Competitive Intelligence*. New York: Simon and Schuster, 1996, p. 17.

Chapter Nine

1. "The Intellgence Community," ibid.
2. "Affidavit in Support of Complaint, Arrest Warrant and Search Warrants: United States v. Harold J. Nicholson." Federal Bureau of Investigation. www.washingtonpost.com/wp-srv/national/long term/ciaspy/affidavt.html.
3. "Affidavit in Support of Complaint, Arrest Warrant and Search Warrants: United States v. Harold J. Nicholson," ibid.
4. Loeb, Vernon, and Brooke A. Master. "Spy Suspect Had Deep Data Access, Ex-Associates Say." *Washington Post*. February 22, 2001, p. A01.
5. Wise, ibid, p. 120.
6. Wise, ibid, p. 118.
7. Wise, ibid, p. 253.
8. Wise, ibid, p. 253.
9. "Rationalizing Treason: An Interview with Aldrich Ames," ibid.

Chapter Ten

1. Mendez, Antonio J., with Malcolm McConnell. *The Master of Disguise: My Secret Life in the CIA*. New York: William Morrow and Company, 1999, p. 31.
2. Redmond, Paul. "America Pays the Price of Openness." *Wall Street Journal*. June 23, 2000, p. A18.
3. Ensor, David. "Spy Agency Tells Congress It Is Breaking No Law." CNN. February 29, 2000. www.cnn.com/2000/US/02/29/echelon.spy/index.html.
4. McKay, Niall. "Lawmakers Raise Questions About International Spy Network." *The New York Times*. May 27, 1999. www.nytimes.com/library/tech/99/05/cyber/articles/27network.html.

5. Love, Alice Ann. "NSA Defends Eavesdropping Policy." Associated Press. February 27, 2000. dailynews.yahoo.com/htx/ap/20000227/pl/government_eavesdropping_2.html.

6. "ACLU Wants FBI to Detail E-Mail Snooper Bureau Using Software to Scan Suspects' Messages." APB News. July 15, 2000. www.apbnews.com/newscenter/breakingnews/2000/07/15/fbis-noop0715_01.html?s=nav_bn_homepage.

7. Johnson, ibid, p. 72.

8. Pincus, Walter and Dan Eggen, "New Powers Sought for Surveillance", *The New York Times*, September 17, 2001, p. AO1.

Chapter Eleven

1. Johnson, ibid, p. 49.

2. Drogin, Bob. "CIA puts the intelligence back into spying." July 7, 2000. www.smh.com.au:80/news/0007/25/text/world12.html.

3. Hughes, Patrick M. "Global Threats and Challenges to the United States and Its Interests Abroad." Defense Intelligence Agency. February 6, 1997. www.loyola.edu/dept/politics/intel/threats.html.

4. Hulnick, ibid, p. 109.

5. Gannon, John C. "The CIA in the New World Order: Intelligence Challenges Through 2015." February 1, 2000. www.cia.gov/cia/public_affairs/speeches/dci_speech_020200smithson.html.

6. Hughes, ibid.

7. Fialka, ibid, p. 107.

8. Fialka, ibid, p. 105.

9. Hedley, John. "Checklist for the Future of Intelligence." Institute for the Study of Diplomacy. 1995. sfswww.georgetown.edu/sfs/programs/isd/files/intell.htm.

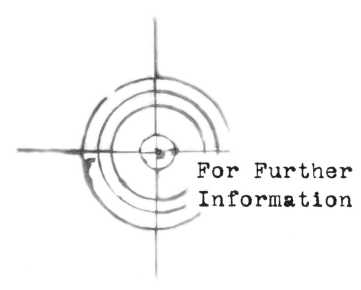

For Further Information

Books

Dux, Frank. *The Secret Man*. New York: ReganBooks, 1996. Autobiography of a CIA covert operations agent.

Lowenthal, Mark. *Intelligence: From Secrets to Policy*. Washington, D.C.: Congressional Quarterly Press, 2000. An overview of the modern U.S. intelligence community, written by a former intelligence agency official.

Melton, H. Keith. *The Ultimate Spy Book*. New York: DK Publishing, Inc., 1996. All about the equipment that spies use, with detailed photographs and diagrams.

Platt, Phillip. *Spy*. New York: Eyewitness Books, 1996. Another book about espionage gadgets with detailed illustrations.

Polmar, Norman. *The Encyclopedia of Espionage*. New York: Random House, 1997. Entries about spies, secret agencies, and spy gadgets.

Richelson, Jeffrey T. *A Century of Spies*. New York: Oxford University Press, 1995. An inside history of intelligence gathering, espionage, and covert activity during the last century.

Schulsky, Abram. *Silent Warfare: Understanding the World of Intelligence*. McLean, VA: Brassey's, Inc., 1991. A close look at the world of spies and spying.

Shirley, Edward G. "Can't Anybody Here Play This Game?" *Atlantic Monthly*. February, 1998. www.theatlantic.com/issues/98feb/cia.htm. A critical look at the Central Intelligence Agency.

Volkman, Ernest. *Spies: The Secret Agents Who Changed the Course of History*. New York: John Wiley and Sons, 1997. Profiles of 45 spies who made espionage history.

On the Internet

The Central Intelligence Agency (CIA)
www.cia.gov
This government agency is responsible for conducting espionage activities in nations outside U.S. borders. Use the site's search for an extensive list of articles about intelligence and espionage.

The Federal Bureau of Investigation (FBI)
www.fbi.gov
The FBI is responsible for tracking down spies within U.S. borders. Use this site's search engine to find thousands of articles on espionage.

The National Security Agency (NSA)
www.nsa.gov
This government agency is responsible for intercepting and analyzing intelligence to detect any potential threats to U.S. national security. See this site's special section entitled "NSA's Cryptologic History."

The Literature of Intelligence
intellit.muskingum.edu/intellsite/maintoc.html
This site is a collection of links to other sites that deal with different aspects of espionage and intelligence. Its coverage is both well-organized and wide-ranging.

Yahoo News: Espionage
search.news.yahoo.com/search/news?p=espionage&c=fullcov&n=10
This Web site supplies links to current news items about espionage and spying, updated daily.

Special Operations.Com
www.specialoperations.com/Intelligence/military.htm
This site contains links to other sites and documents about military intelligence, including covert operations.

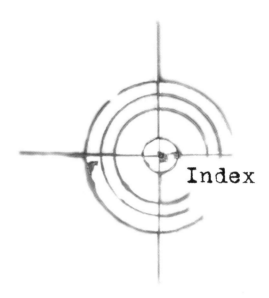

Index

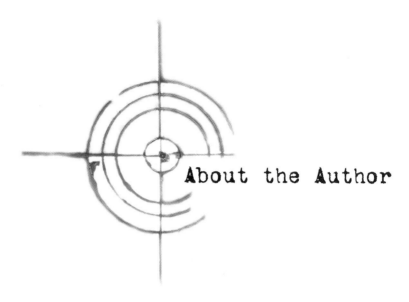

About the Author

Ron Fridell has been writing since his college days at Northwestern University, where he earned a Master's Degree in Radio, TV, Film. He has written for radio, TV, newspapers, and textbooks. He taught English as a second language while a member of the Peace Corps in Bangkok, Thailand. He lives in the Midwest with his wife, Patricia, and their dog, an Australian shepherd named Madeline.